KU-360-197

CONTENTS

GRANNY WAS A BROTHEL KEEPER

Introduction by Kate Broad

This book is not an instruction manual for people wanting to research their family history. Between us, Toni and I have around 45 years experience in genealogy and along the way, have made errors, omissions, incorrect assumptions and generally cocked it up. Now, whilst definitely not perfect, we have honed our skills so that our mistakes are thankfully few and far between, and our aim here is to show you, the reader, what the banana-skins of family history can be and how to avoid skidding and landing on your backside, metaphorically speaking. By using stories, cartoons, tips and personal comments in a light-hearted style, we aim to help beginners get things right first time, and introduce methods and techniques to old-timers that could take them by surprise.

We decided to write this book because to our knowledge, no one has attempted anything similar. Most books on family history are packed full of useful information, but they seem to miss the opportunities to show just how silly, bizarre, unexpected and laugh-out-loud it can be. The majority of the stories in this book are true; although sometimes names have been left out to protect the innocent.

Collaborations between people to write books are never easy. There are, no doubt, many promising starts which have come to nothing, simply because the authors have fallen out due to artistic differences or since they cannot agree where a comma should go in a particular sentence. Had we known at the beginning how long it might take us to get to the stage where we were ready to publish, we might have decided to do something easier.

There have been highs and lows in writing this book, and its follow up, "Grandad Was A Dwarf Strangler: 50 More Family History Traps", but our long friendship, together with our shared sense of humour and lashings of Toni's home-made soup, have kept us going. The anticipation we felt every time we wrote something that might make the other laugh would spur us on; and the gratification we got when that happened gave us a warm glow inside.

We hope you have as much fun reading this as we have had putting it together.

Our thanks go to:
Our long-suffering families who have had to put up with prolonged absences, no food in the house, stories told about them, late meals or just the general lack of our smiling faces; Colin Piggott and James Ditton for Norfolk weekends plus technical and practical help and advice; Jim Wilkins for turning our ideas into brilliant illustrated reality; Rob Cole for advice and support; Jackie Ford for proof reading and use of a family story; Tim Neobard for technical advice; Bill Neobard for proof reading and content suggestions; and people who have let us use their family stories; Julie Pavitt; Keith & Lynette Martin; Tony Acott; Helen Neobard & the Davis family; Sue Acott; Carol Nubbert; Betty Hitchcock; and Gary Cremer.

✳✳✳

Lastly ..... about the abbreviations used in the book. We have tried not to use too many of them as we find them annoying, but we couldn't avoid including a few. These are:

BMD: Births, Marriages & Deaths
GRO: General Register Office
LDS: Refers to The Church of Jesus Christ of Latter Day Saints who provide a great deal of genealogical material to the public, both on-line and through their Family Search Centres

SECTION 1

LIES, DAMN LIES AND FAMILY RECOLLECTIONS

Problems with using your relatives as a family history resource

"In my expert opinion your grandad's medals were not for saving a comrade's life, but for saving sufficient Bellog's Cornflakes tokens"

Trap 1. You start with unrealistic expectations

You ask anyone who is researching their family history why they are embarking on this engrossing and time-consuming hobby and they will give you a number of reasons, such as, "I want to know where I come from", or "I was interested to know what my ancestors did". Some people may even have a family story they want to confirm or they may have been inspired by a television programme. Scratch below the surface, however, and you may find secret hopes of murderers, lost wealth, exotic ancestry or royal connections. Certainly such exciting stories exist for some lucky individuals, but there is a greater chance that you are descended from a line of agricultural labourers stretching as far back as you can go. It is possible to spend countless hours of research time and not even discover the theft of a sheep or whiff of illegitimacy to liven up your family tree. But with a bit of persistence you may be able to find nuggets of information to fatten up those skeletons, metaphorically speaking!

> **Toni's tip:** *Family history should be more than just names and dates on a chart. Try to flesh out individual lives – talking to elderly relatives can be a rich source for this, at least for a couple of generations back.*

A perfect illustration of where expectations fall short is with some research we were carrying out for a client, whose family name was 'Doncaster'. It was well known within the family that they used to live in Clerkenwell, in London, in an area known as Little Italy. It was called Little Italy as there had been a large Italian population there; immigrants who arrived from around 1880 onwards. The client wanted to find out more about his family story, which indicated that he was descended from an Italian family whose name was something like "Casta". Being the head of the family, the ancestor was known as 'Don' Casta and the name had been anglicised to 'Doncaster'. His wife said that after a glass or two of Chianti he liked to muse on his potential mafia connections. We suspected he also had hopes of family connections to a nice part of Tuscany and had visions of summer holidays in Italy to check out the old family village.

It is an entertaining story but it seems to be untrue. Certainly the family did at one time live in Little Italy but we were able to follow the Doncaster line back to the mid 1700s to various parts of London, far too early for the bulk of the Italian immigration to the UK. Quite a few of his ancestors worked as tennis equipment makers but that looks like the only 'racketeering' the family was involved in! It turned out that the Doncaster family had been fairly well-to-do and had owned several properties around London, including a coffee house in Soho. Some of these properties still exist today but we recognise that a day trip to London isn't quite as exciting as a trip to Tuscany to see the old family home.

Kate's comment: This is your own detective story and a huge part of the enjoyment in seeking out your family roots is found in the actual process of research. That ecstatic feeling of finally solving the missing link you have been struggling with for ages is hard to beat. If you are tracing your family in the hopes that you may discover family money then you are very likely to be disappointed. But what you might find along the way is that you feel you are getting to know these people you have been researching so diligently and may perhaps wonder whether you would have liked them had you ever met them.

Trap 2. You just didn't get around to it in time

How about the following true story, guaranteed to break a family historian's heart? After the death of her husband, Mrs X went to live with one of her children. Before the move, she decided to get rid of all that old clutter that had been hanging around for years. She threw away not just his false teeth but also cards, certificates and pictures and sold her husband's first-world-war medals. When this was discovered some time later, she expressed surprise that anyone else could have been in the slightest bit interested in that old rubbish, although admitted that the teeth could have come in handy. We didn't find out how they could be of use – perhaps she had designs on the dentally-challenged widower next door. Of course, what she did still have intact was her memories, a valuable resource for the family historian to tap into. With any older relatives, you need to talk to them before it is too late.

Kate's comment: Due to a family falling-out, my father only met his grandmother once, and that was when an uncle took him to meet her. The problem is, no one ever asked why the family quarrelled and now it is too late – the protagonists have departed this world and we will probably never know what was behind it. It must have been serious to cause such a major rift.

Family recollection has the potential to be one of the most important sources of information there is, as it can take you to places that written records alone cannot do. Arrange to visit the older members of your family and even take advantage of family events such as weddings or funerals to see what they can remember. Sometimes older people are a bit reluctant to give away what they might regard as 'secrets' but after a glass of sherry or two they may be more inclined to reminisce – although we are certainly not suggesting you deliberately get Great Aunt Maud legless just to get her to shed some light on the murkier aspects of your family's past.

Kate's comment: *It is usually the case that the older the relative, the further back in time they are likely to be able to take you. It is also the case that the older they are, the shorter the amount of time they are likely to be around so if you are thinking of starting your family history, or you have made a start but are getting a bit stuck, go and visit your sick or elderly relatives before it is too late! Once they are gone their vast repositories of memories are gone with them, so perhaps it's time to get a move on!*

Margaret was surprised to learn that her grand-mother wasn't a hat maker from Chipping Norton, as the records had indicated, but was a burlesque dancer from Camden.

For those of you who really didn't get round to it in time, there does exist at least one family history research service that specialises in tracing your roots though the use of a Medium. They offer to make contact with your ancestors who have 'gone beyond the veil'. Whilst we agree that being able to talk directly to our dear departed ones would cut out an awful lot of work, we leave it to the reader to decide on the merits of such methods.

Toni's tips for interviewing relatives: *When you are interviewing your relatives, it is important that you have a record of what they say.*

❋ *Either record the conversation or take someone with you to write down details as you talk. It is worth doing this for aspects of the conversation which at the time don't seem particularly important – often they aren't important but sometimes they may hold the key to understanding later research. This is particularly true of family stories.*

❋ *If recording, its best to make sure your equipment is fully charged or you have spare batteries.*

❋ *Your relatives may be suspicious of your motives – let them know why you want the information and keep them informed of what you subsequently discover. This may trigger new memories or further details.*

❋ *Don't expect to get everything you need from one meeting at a social event. Use the occasion to make arrangements to meet again.*

❋ *Make sure your relative knows how to contact you, as it's a safe bet that as soon as you have waved goodbye and turned around the corner, he or she will be remembering something else that you should know. Even better, see if you can persuade them to write these extra memories out for you.*

Transcribe your notes or recordings as soon as you can. This allows you time to go back to your relative for clarification on any misunderstood points

Trap 3. Family memories are muddled

Talk to any police officer about the reliability of witness testimonies and they are likely to be amused at the concept. To illustrate this, at a recent investigation into an air crash witnessed by several hundred people, some 52% of witnesses noted that the aeroplane had been on fire before it crashed; 48% either didn't notice this fact or had forgotten it. All of these people were interviewed very soon after the event. If nearly half of the witnesses were unable to report accurately on such a major and distinctive event, imagine the possibilities for forgetting or muddling information about long-dead relatives.

So don't expect your relatives to be able to be wholly accurate when discussing family. Also don't discount the possibility that your family members are completely barking mad and you won't ever get sense from them! However, assuming that they are not away with the fairies, information that you are given may still be muddled. For example, you may well get told that Great Auntie Jessie was your father's father's sister, whereas she turns out to be your father's mother's sister. People may not even know the relationship – people known as, for example, aunts, just known by their first names, may turn out to be friends of the family or aunts by marriage. Unless your interviewee knows distant relatives well enough to send them Christmas cards, they may not have a clue about their surnames.

> *Toni's tip:* Make a rough draft of a family tree as you go along to show the person who is reminiscing. This may help them clarify who is related to whom and to remind them of further details that could be of use to you. Interview brothers and sisters separately as well as together. Interviewing them together may trigger memories in each other but on the other hand they may argue about details. When separate they may give you information they don't want their siblings to know about.

Often some memories are crystal clear and others somewhat hazy. Kate has been told over the years that the male line on one side of the family consisted variously of Irish tinkers, Welsh drovers, and more latterly that they originated from Exeter in Devon. Kate's mum had visited Exeter and had found it had felt surprisingly familiar to her, even though she had never visited it before. Kate's mum was told that her paternal line came from there, so it was obviously some kind of inherited 'memory' of the place. In more recent years, Kate has taken this line back to around 1790, and found that this line were in the main agricultural labourers, all from Wiltshire. No evidence of Irish, Welsh or definitely no Devon ancestry exists during this time. Kate could have spent a lot of time trying to link in ancestors from these areas but there is every possibility that her mum had got it muddled or had been on the receiving end of jokes that have been taken seriously.

Surprisingly, however, Kate found that when looking at her mum's maternal line, that they came from, you've guessed it, Exeter, and the surname was Williams – so further work may find that there are indeed Welsh drovers somewhere in the line – but there are as yet no Irish tinkers.

Trap 4. Family recollections lead you astray

You will always have one family member who is adamant that nuggets of information they give you are the absolute, god-given truth. Be wary of people who are convinced they know the facts as they are often mistaken!

"Your Great Uncle Robert was always helping
the police to solve crimes"

One friend of the authors remembers talking to her mother about her mother's Aunt Lucinda who lived next door to the family when she was growing up. The mother (called Mary, a young girl in the 1950s) remembered Aunt Lucinda in fascinating detail – not surprisingly, as she seemed quite a colourful character. As far as Mary was aware, Lucinda was not married and had a number of distinguishing features, including always wearing men's clothes and smoking cigars. She was extraordinarily fond of animals and always kept several dogs and cats, usually strays picked up in her travels, or some which just turned up at her door.

Apparently she became extremely upset when any of the animals died, to such an extent that she could not bear to have them buried but instead would take the poor bodies to a taxidermist and get them stuffed and mounted so she would always have them with her.

As the years went by, the collection grew, and when Mary was in her teens she remembers that if you visited her it was becoming difficult to move around parts of the house because of the sheer number of the departed. Strangely, she often had a group seated around the dining table to be with her when she ate. In the later years, some of the stuffed animals started to look distinctly moth-eaten and battered where the living animals had scratched or attacked them, and the house took on a rather unpleasant smell. In the end, Lucinda became too old to care for herself properly and was moved into a residential home. As a result she had to leave her collection behind, which was probably destroyed. Mary didn't see her again but believed she pined away because of missing her beloved pets.

What a wonderful eccentric to have in the family, and what fun you could have telling people about your barmy great aunt. Determined to find out a bit more about her life, our friend (with a little help from us) embarked on researching the family with a view to seeing what she could learn. What she learnt was a great surprise. Neither of her grandparents (Mary's parents) had any sisters, nor had any brothers ever married a Lucinda or even anyone close in name. There was no evidence whatsoever of half-sisters, adoptive sisters or any one connected in the family at all called Lucinda. So the sad truth was that Mary was probably told to call someone who was only a neighbour by the name 'Aunt' and she wasn't a real blood relative at all.

> **Toni's tip:** *If a family story looks unlikely, it is probable that elements are embellished. However, don't dismiss it, keep a note of it, sometimes it may contain a grain of truth.*

Trap 5. You don't maximise family information

The more relatives you have, the richer and deeper the sources of information you have. It is important that you get out there and talk to them all, not just once but several times, as exchanging information will lead to yet more stories and facts being opened up to you. Sometimes some details won't seem that exciting to you at the time but may help to clear up mysteries in the future. Even physical descriptions of relatives could potentially have a use in the future as supplements to DNA tests – it could help chart where those blue eyes and blond hair that pop up in the family from time to time come from, especially when nearly everyone in the family has brown eyes and brunette hair. If you do have a distinctive feature in the family, such as ginger hair, it can be fun finding out which ancestors you can blame for this.

Of course, there may be some relatives that are just too far away to visit. You may be living in the UK but have family all around the world, and it may be hard to justify the expense of travelling to Australia just to interview a distant cousin. In these circumstances you could try contacting them by letter or email.

> **Toni's tip:** *If you do write, it is a good idea to ensure you ask suitable questions – perhaps in the form of a questionnaire. Be careful how you phrase your questions, don't just ask something like 'Do you remember Great Uncle Robert' because they may have more than one Great Uncle Robert, or they may simply answer with a 'Yes' or 'No' which won't be of much use. Instead, ask 'What can you tell me about Robert Jones, your Great Uncle on your mother's side,' which gives them better detail of who you mean as well as prompting them to say what they know about him.*

People who have emigrated are often very interested in finding out about their roots and may well be very happy to help on the basis that they can see the results of your work when ready. Ask if they have any relevant photographs and documents that they can scan/email or photocopy/ send to you. You might get a better response if you offer to pay for any out-of-pocket expenses they may have.

When you have amassed sufficient information and have been able to draw up the beginnings of a family tree, you could host a 'family history day' when your relatives can come along and view what you have done so far.

Toni's tip: *If you are thinking of hosting a family history day for your relatives, draw up a tree and get together some boards to display your family photographs and documents. On the day, you can use the time to spark and capture memories and bring the family tree up to date with the names and dates of the newer members. It also gives an opportunity to put names to the unknown faces in photographs.*

Make sure you have a scanner or photocopier available and send out a request with your invitations that guests bring along any photographs, certificates or documents that you haven't yet seen. This will give you the chance to take copies there and then.

At one such occasion, a photograph was shown by a researcher friend to her elderly aunt, which portrayed the aunt's late sister with an unknown man. She was able to tell the surprised researcher that the man had been the sister's first husband and told her:

"They were childhood sweethearts, we grew up together in the same village and they had been friends for years. He joined the Army and was posted to India, where she eventually sailed out to meet him and they were married. It was unfortunately a very short-lived marriage, as within a few months he had con-tracted dysentery and died. She was a widow at 22 and returned home shortly afterwards. She met and married your Uncle Bert about a year later."

This was amazing information because our researcher friend had absolutely no idea that her aunt had been married twice or that she had ever travelled to India! She was later able to confirm the story, having been able to find the registration of her aunt's marriage and details of the aunt's journeys on ship's manifests, going out in her maiden name and returning in her married name, as a widow.

After a relatively short period of time talking to your family, it is surprising just how much material you can gather. Some of it may help you at the outset; but other material may only be significant at a later stage in your researches. Don't ever decide that something is irrelevant just because you cannot immediately fit it into the right place. What is important is that you re-read the information you have on a regular basis and cross-check it against anything new that comes in. That way you will not miss any potential connections.

> **Kate's comment:** Try to acknowledge any help that family members give to you. A simple acknowledgement, with thanks, for any information given to you will go a long way and means that people will be more inclined to help you again in the future.

Trap 6. What they don't want you to know

There are very few families around that can't claim to have at least one skeleton in the cupboard – something that only one generation knew about and did not think it suitable information to pass on to their children. You are very unlikely to find no illegitimacy in any family being researched. It is estimated that at around 50% of Victorian brides (that prim and proper lot) were pregnant when they walked down the aisle. So it is possible that at least one of your ancestors was the major reason for his/her parents getting married. This can lead to marriage or birth dates being 'tweaked' so that decency is upheld – after all, there was no need for anyone outside of immediate family to be aware that Granny and Grandad weren't averse to the odd tumble in the hay before they married!

The problem here for researchers is that you may be told quite categorically that the grandparents married in 1901 and Aunt Gladys was a honeymoon baby born in 1902, whereas dear old Gladys was a bun in the oven when the marriage took place, rather hastily, in 1902. If the grandparents were in possession of a commonplace set of names such as Thomas and Mary Smith, looking for a wedding certificate for the wrong year could lead to a wrong certificate being ordered, which can cost you money and send your research in a misleading direction.

> **Kate's comment:** *These subterfuges can have long-lasting repercussions. For example, a friend of ours was organising a 60th wedding anniversary party for close relatives. Part of the celebrations was going to be a surprise card from the Queen, which can be arranged through Buckingham Palace. In order to do this, it is necessary to supply a copy of the marriage certificate for proof. Unfortunately, a check of the marriage registers revealed that they were actually celebrating their 59th wedding anniversary! The family were too embarrassed to say anything so the 60th celebrations went ahead, minus the Queen's endorsement.*

Take this following true example from Toni's family. Great Granny was the kind of person who could be described as 'a paragon of virtue.' She was a decent, respectable hard-working woman who attended church regularly and brought up her children to follow a strict moral code. Some time after her death, her family decided to track down her roots and – I expect you are ahead of us here – found to their surprise that the great-grandparents' date of marriage was a year later than everyone had believed, in 1911, and she had been seven months pregnant with the grandfather at the time.

> **Toni's tip:** *Treat family information about birth and marriage dates with caution, unless you have some concrete evidence such as birth, marriage and death certificates. Often the day and month may be correct but the year can be suspect, and very likely to be a year out in the case of marriages.*

When the 1911 census became available to view, a further shock was in store. The family had assumed that the happy couple had at least lived in the same area before marrying. However, it turned out that at the date of the census (when she would have been four months pregnant) she was living and working as a servant in a vicarage two whole counties away from where her future husband was living and working. It was at this point that the family remembered how they all used to comment on how strange it was that their short, weedy grandfather looked nothing like their tall, strapping great grandfather – they are now wondering what the vicar had looked like!

Returning from his long tour of duty John was delighted to find he'd become a father.

Trap 7. Families make assumptions about what you know

It is a fairly recent phenomenon that children are included in discussions of, shall we say, a more intimate nature than the older generation would have been comfortable with. There are far less taboos in conversation today than there were even 20 or 30 years ago. If a family in the past had a delicate matter to discuss they would often talk in some kind of code or use a euphemism for the subject matter in order that the children could be 'sheltered' from the harsh facts of adult life. This is quite understandable but it does mean that you may grow up completely oblivious to something that the rest of the family are well aware of. Yet in later life the same family may be completely taken aback because you do not know something that the rest of them do – they make the assumption that because they know, and that you are now an adult, you must know it as well.

Take this phrase which used to be in common use: 'going to see a man about a dog.' It was a polite way of telling someone to mind their own business. For example, if a curious child asked where an older relative was going, he may have responded with that phrase deliberately to avoid letting the child know what he was actually doing. He could simply be going for a hospital appointment, or to buy Christmas presents, or maybe doing some dodgy deals down the local pub. You as a child may just register the concept of 'dog' and grow up with the vague belief that Uncle Mick was some kind of dog trainer or breeder! It would probably come as a bit of a surprise to discover much later that he was a career criminal with convictions for fencing stolen goods.

Toni's tip: *Your relatives need to be encouraged to talk about the mundane as well as the interesting. It can be helpful to ask targeted questions to draw out the maximum information, such as "Can you tell me all the different jobs that Uncle Bob had.".*

Here's a story from Toni's researches that we hope illustrates the ease in which family members assume that just because they know something, everyone in the family knows it:

"So there we were, the family around the table, idly chatting after our Sunday lunch. At that point, I was a veteran of around 30 years of family history research and I felt confident that I knew practically all that there was to know about a fair number of preceding generations. I had produced family trees and had even used family gatherings to share the fruits of my labours with aunts, uncles, cousins, second cousins and so on and had always taken note of any stories or information that these relatives had to give me.

"We were discussing my Grandfather on my mother's side, who was unfortunately named 'John Thomas Bradley'. I could remember from conversations with my mum that he had worked for most of his life at Bretons Farm, in Essex. His marriage certificate had described his occupation as 'Farm Worker' so I had automatically assumed that, like preceding generations, he was an agricultural labourer. I imagined him following the horse-drawn plough; forking the hay onto the wain; the wind in his hair and the sun on his weather-beaten brow. So I asked my mum what he had done on the farm. My parents looked at me in surprise.

"Didn't you realise," said mum, "you only lived just down the road from it. Bretons Farm was a sewage farm." "Yes", chipped in dad, "your grandfather wasn't a farmer, he was a sh*t shoveller! Mind you, he always had a lovely crop of tomatoes!" When Toni then asked why no one had put her straight at family gatherings when her research had been on display for all to see, the response was "Well, we thought you could have been embarrassed about Grandad's job and didn't want anyone to know what he did…"

Kate's comment: Toni may not have found this out without the chance conversation which revealed the true nature of her grandad's job. Toni's relatives had always known that Bretons Farm had been a sewage farm and had simply assumed that she knew that too, especially as she lived a short distance from it.

Trap 8. Relatives sanitise their recollections

If we are lucky enough to find something 'juicy' in our family, for example, a family member transported to Australia because of the theft of a pie, or hung for highway robbery, this gives us something interesting to talk about. If our families were all dressmakers or general labourers it can be a bit of a disappointment. One of Kate's female ancestors was described in 1822 by her Vicar as "A loose and immoral woman" which is highly entertaining, now that we are almost 200 years after the event. How she or her nearest and dearest felt about being described thus is not recorded. However, if something scandalous or upsetting occurred in more recent times then your family members might not be so happy to have details of this discussed and dissected for all to consider.

> *Toni's tip:* If something momentous or unusual has happened to a recent family member, it is a good idea to seek sources of information other than from those close to that person. Try newspaper archives or talking to someone from the same generation but who is not directly involved – perhaps a relative by marriage, a neighbour or friend of the family.

When Toni was growing up she was aware that a tragedy had occurred in her family involving her father's cousin, Robert Wilsden. She had been told that he was the driver of a train which derailed and he had died as a result. Toni was led to believe that it was just an unfortunate accident. However, there was more to it than the family let on, and Toni was able to discover the non-sanitised story in the report of the official enquiry into the crash.

In 1972, aged just 33, Robert was a train driver. In June of that year he drove a train which derailed near Eltham Station. The full truth was that Robert had been drinking heavily on the day of the crash before starting work, and continued to do so whilst in charge of the train. Post-mortem examinations found him to be almost 10 times over the present-day drink-driving limit. He drove his train around the bend before Eltham at 65 mph, ignoring the 20 mph speed limit in operation at that time, causing the derailment. Six people died, including Robert, and a further 126 were injured.

Kate's comment: You can hardly blame the relatives for wanting to sanitise this story. No right thinking person would want others to know that they have someone in their family who was completely to blame for causing death, injury and distress to so many people, because of their drinking. Of course, not many people are going to have this kind of story in their family but if something has occurred which is felt to be shameful or embarrassing, then you as researcher may be given something that puts the perpetrator into a better light and have the less pleasant considerations glossed over or even lied about.

Sometimes the events in a family are so bad or momentous that no traces of these have been passed down in the family even through the direct line, and the tale of the Pavitt family makes us see why.

Our researches took us back to George and Ann Pavitt who lived in London during the 19th century. George had been a policeman in the force's formative years and as such could reasonably be expected to be of good character and honest occupation. Indeed, he featured as witness in a number of Old Bailey trials, including helping to convict known brothel-keepers. It came as a surprise, then, to find him in 1855 being held in the Debtor's prison and appearing in the Insolvency Court. To be fair, he was being held not in his own right, but for a debt run up by his wife, Ann. She had been convicted of falsely accusing her brother-in-law and owed £60 as a result.

Further research showed Ann to be somewhat of a career criminal. She had been accused and convicted variously of perjury, receiving stolen property, slander and bigamy. She was known for her reckless swearing and bad language. At one point she was called "Mother Pavitt" because she had exhorted poor children to plunder and steal for her. A description of her from one court case held her to be "a short, very fat and vulgar looking woman." There was even a mocking song about her conviction entitled "The Cable Street Perjury" being sold and sung in the streets of London.

In February 1862 things took on a more unsavoury note, when Ann was up before the Thames Court to answer summons on the assault of a 17-year old servant girl. Ann and George had been running a business described as a 'refreshment and wine rooms' but that in reality was a brothel. Mrs Pavitt had told the newly employed young servant girl to serve the sailors in the back room. The type of 'serving' envisaged was not so innocent and the sailors acted with great indecency towards the young girl who screamed for help. But Ann was holding the door shut so that her latest recruit could not escape. To add further insult, Ann even tried to accuse the girl of stealing from her. The judge at the trial was quoted as saying that "Mrs Pavitt is, without exception, the most wicked woman I ever saw in the whole course of my life" and had no qualms in sentencing her to imprisonment in the House of Correction for two months of hard labour.

A few months later, both George and Ann were indicted and sentenced for brothel keeping. It was clear that the police were called many times to the house. It was also alleged that their own children, one of them a 14-year old girl, took part in the scenes "which were daily and nightly enacted...." On this occasion both Ann and George were sentenced to six months hard labour and a £50 fine.

So with ancestors like this, it comes as little surprise that stories about them had not been passed down through the generations. Not many people would be pleased and delighted at the thought of having a brothel keeper in the family; especially one as notorious as Mrs Pavitt!

Of course, the Great Aunts in Portsmouth were very prim & proper.

Trap 9. Taking it at face value

It is a truth universally acknowledged (apologies to Ms Austen) that a story in the telling is in receipt of a degree of embellishment at each recounting. As children, if we are given the opportunity, we love to sit and listen to stories told to us by our parents and grandparents. Such stories are often 'handed down' through the generations, so that stories told to you by grandparents may have in turn been told to them by their parents and subsequently you may pass them on to the next generation

But what does this mean to the family historian? Certainly one of the most enjoyable things about researching your family history is the chance to use family stories to build up a picture of those who have gone before, but after all the additions and deletions given to each story, the tale may not reflect an accurate picture of the people at all. So the moral of this story is to treat family stories with a degree of caution, but bear in mind that often there is a grain of truth hidden in there somewhere.

> *Kate's comment:* Family stories can be a bit like the children's game, Chinese Whispers. On each retelling, the stories are 'tweaked' – modified to suit the story telling style of the teller and to make it more interesting to the listener. Events may be added to, embellished or glossed over completely in order to make the story more listenable. Each and every one of us is likely to be guilty of doing this.

Toni has a tale which illustrates this very well:

"When I was young, I was told by my father about an ancestor who had been shipwrecked. Apparently the poor soul was adrift at sea on a small boat for four days and four nights with four lascars (East Indian sailors) and a cabin boy. After a couple of days aboard with nothing to eat and nothing to drink but salt water they became addled and one of the brutish lascars stated that he was going to kill and eat the cabin boy. However, my heroic ancestor said that if the boy was harmed, he would tip up the boat and drown them all."

Well, who wouldn't want a hero like that in the family? So Toni decided to investigate to see if she could find out more detail about the family superman. She started by talking to one of her great-aunts who was able to tell her that the story related to her grandfather, Benjamin Sheals (Toni's great-great-grandfather). The ship that sank was called 'The London' and she remembered the date as it coincided with her birthday, 11th January, but she did not know which year. She was also convinced that the sinking took place in the Bristol Channel.

"I then spoke to my other surviving great-aunt, her sister, who stated quite categorically that the ship concerned had been a passenger liner on its way to Australia and that nearly everyone on board had drowned. She also dismissed the idea of it being in the Bristol Channel – as far as she was concerned it had happened in the Bay of Biscay! She did, however, agree that it was on her sister's birth date (11th January) but again could not confirm the year.

"This was rapidly turning into a much bigger story than I had anticipated. These new details gave me the breakthrough I needed. The Internet provided me with the first big lead, which was an article written about the 'SS London' which had sunk in the Bay of Biscay during a hurricane on the 11th January 1866."

Subsequent research was able to throw up a wealth of material on this sinking, as this story was the 'Titanic' of its day, since around 220 people had died, with only 19 survivors picked up. The Times newspaper had almost a hundred articles on the incident, with reports appearing frequently in the paper in the following months, including daily bulletins from the official enquiry into the sinking. These reports confirmed that Toni's great-great-grandfather had been one of the survivors, but did the facts match the family story?

"My great-great-grandfather does seem to have been a bit of a hero. He certainly had a strong sense for survival! Despite being injured during the run up to the sinking, he had crawled back on deck and together with another member of the crew, had managed to persuade the captain to turn the ship to give a bit of shelter which would enable a lifeboat to be launched. There had already been one failed attempt to launch a lifeboat which resulted in the boat smashing against the side of the ship. This next attempt had been successful but attempts to get the passengers into the lifeboat failed as they were too afraid to make the transfer into the smaller boat. However, my great-great-grandfather, together with a few of the crew, decided to take their chances and go for it. The official enquiry reports how the lifeboat had just managed to move clear of the London when it sank rapidly."

So if you compare the facts with the family story – there were 19 on board the lifeboat, not six, although one of the 19 was indeed a cabin boy. They were adrift for 18 hours – not the four days and nights as told to Toni. If the sailors were addled, it wasn't through drinking seawater; it was more likely due to drinking the bottles of wine and spirits that they had taken on board with them. And as to the threat of eating the cabin boy – it is hard to imagine the sailors being crazed with hunger considering there was about a hundredweight of ship's biscuits on board.

So all in all, a first-class family story with a sufficient 'grain of truth' to lead Toni to a fascinating part of her family's history.

> **Toni's tip:** When looking into family stories, look out for any potential facts, such as a link to someone's birthday or anniversary. They may be accurately remembered.

Trap 10. You neglect recent family recollections

The aspect of family history research which captures most first-time researchers is the drive to go back to as early a date as possible. When you discuss with other people what you are doing, usually the opening gambit of the conversation is "I've managed to get the family back to 1740 or thereabouts", only to be upstaged by "Oh, we go back to 1675" or similar. We know one person who was disappointed that their family could only be traced back to 1590! Certainly once you have exhausted all possible sources for each line of your family, it is quite possible to sit back, look at your family tree and enjoy the fruits of your labours. However, if you do this, you could be missing out on some fascinating aspects of your family's more recent history. We have already talked about investigating family stories and trying to get some detail on those, but this section will deal with the joys of capturing facts about people you may actually know or have known.

There are two principal reasons why you should consider going down this route. Firstly, because these stories may only be one or two generations away, they are likely to be remembered with a great deal more accuracy than tales of longer ago. Secondly, as the years go by these stories will of themselves become those of long ago and will hopefully be of great interest to the generations to come. There is a great deal of interest in 'living history' with projects around the country to record recollections, archive letters and reports. Schools now invite elderly locals to talk to children about their own experiences during the Second World War, such as being child evacuees, rationing, make-do-and-mend, working in ammunitions factories and even, if the children are lucky, to hear about the day the narrator captured an enemy pilot!

> ***Toni's tip:*** *A useful tool is looking at old photographs with an elderly relative. The photographs can help prompt interesting memories. Wedding photographs are often very useful as they may show more distant relatives, first husbands that you didn't know about or interesting people the family were friendly with.*

So what can be better than capturing your own family members' stories about their experiences? Take this example, where two brothers, Tony and Ronnie, got into trouble as children during the Second World War. A casual request as to why Ronnie only had stumps for fingers prompted this tale from Tony:

"Ronnie and I had been scavenging on a crashed German aircraft on the banks of the Thames. We were first on the scene and the wreck was complete with a dead airman. We knew we had to be quick because as soon as the authorities got there we would have been sent away fast, maybe even with a clip around the ear! So when we found lots of lovely 30mm cannon shells and various 9mm 303 bullets, we took them back to our house before they could be confiscated. When mum saw one of the shells, she asked us what it was – Ronnie could always think fast so he told her it was a bicycle pump. He took the ammo into the shed and put one of the cannon shells into the vice. He took it apart, carefully putting the cordite into matchboxes, and he was poking the gun cotton out of the fuse with a nail when the shell exploded. This blew the windows out of the shed and propelled his fingers onto the lawn.

"An ambulance was called, and his fingers retrieved and given to the ambulance crew. However, because refrigeration was not readily available then, they had deteriorated too far to be able to reattach. This event had an amazing effect on the local population – the next few days found the local ARP wardens inundated with thousands of rounds of ammunition, shells, bombs and the like which had been handed in by residents in the district once the word had gone around!"

Kate's comment: I know of people who kept incredibly detailed diaries of wartime experiences or just their general day to day lives. It is worthwhile asking around the family to find if anything like this is kept within the family. You may be worried that you are reading things 'personal' to that individual which is difficult if you have your own memories of that person (what, our grandparents had a love life?) but you may have a rich source of detail about, for example, their jobs or homes, friends and neighbours or even what they liked to eat!

Perhaps you could consider writing your own memoirs. Your grandchildren might be fascinated to see how their grandparents lived their lives, how they coped without mobile phones and what passed for entertainment when they were younger. But maybe leave out the details of the knee-trembler you had behind the Romford Odeon that resulted in their mother coming along.

CHAOS IS NOT JUST A THEORY

Getting organised

"To my nephew Eric, the family historian, I bequeath my shopping receipts from the last 72 years, that should keep him quiet for a while."

Trap 11. Your workspace doesn't work for you

You might think that the amount of paperwork and equipment needed to effectively undertake family history research would be minimal and that it would be a nice, cheap hobby that you can fit in around your other commitments. You may believe that a notebook and pencil would be sufficient but before long you will find that your requirements extend to a file to keep your material in, then increasing into a bookshelf, a computer, a cupboard, a room, a small house – or at least an extension on the existing one. If you live on your own in a large clutter-free house with plenty of available storage, then this section probably isn't for you, but if you are one of the vast majority of us who live in smaller houses with rooms that have multiple functions, then you may well have to vie for space with partners, children, homework, ironing piles, junk mail, bills, or goats.

The key to all this, of course, is to be organised. Sifting through heaps of papers for items that you need is, as we all know, time-wasting and irritating but it isn't readily appreciated just how much that disorganisation can seriously affect your lifestyle. For example, a global pharmaceutical company carried out research into this subject, and discovered that women who live in chaos are significantly more likely to become pregnant by accident than those who are organised.

So in order to carry out your research efficiently (and perhaps to avoid unwanted pregnancies) we would suggest, as a basic minimum, that you have a large clear surface on which you can work with open folders, spread-out documents and large family trees. You should also have available a bookshelf or cupboard which is easily accessible and large enough to accommodate your future requirements. If you look at your storage space and decide you will never fill that with your

Adapting the workspace to suit your changing needs.

family history stuff, think again. Go for something at least twice as big, you'll need it. Easy access to your material is also important, as it can be de-motivating to have to climb into the loft or have to move the vacuum cleaner or crates of wine in order to get to it.

> **Toni's tip:** *If you want to maintain domestic harmony in your household and avoid complaints that your hobby is taking over everyone's lives, put away your papers after each session. You will also avoid having your important documents handled by sticky-fingered children.*

Having your workspace and storage close to your computer is handy, as is having a drawer for stationery and scrap paper. If you don't have a computer at home but are using facilities elsewhere, such as libraries, then we wouldn't suggest you carry everything around with you, only take copies of what you really need in case you leave it on the bus.

> **Kate's comment:** *One other item to mention is that it can be very disruptive if you are trying to sort out all your information and you get a constant stream of people into your work room, asking for such things like clean socks or have you seen their car keys. It helps if you can pre-arrange a set time whereby people in your household are aware that you are busy and will leave you alone until you finish. Having a set time for your hobby helps to prevent you becoming obsessive with it, too!*

And for those of you who are chronically disorganised and are beginning to lose hope that you will be successful in your endeavours, we would like to offer a crumb of comfort. If it hadn't been for his lack of organisational skills, a certain young scientist, investigating the bacterium staphylococci, would not have left a petri dish containing cultures of the bacteria on a bench whilst he went on holiday, only to discover on his return that a fungus had developed and had destroyed a culture. Had he tidied this away before he disappeared, then Alexander Fleming would not have discovered penicillin.

Trap 12. Your findings are disorganised

Having dealt with the orderliness or otherwise of your workspace, its now time to consider how you order your findings. Being messy may aid creativity and adaptability but this is unlikely to help the family historian. From experience we have found that keeping family papers in good logical order avoids repeating the same searches and makes it easy to lay your hands on important documents when you want them. With the sort of busy lives that people commonly have now, any time that you can dedicate to your hobbies is precious.

Shoving everything into a folder will be fine at first, but eventually you will have so much information that a single folder will not be enough and a little organisation right at the very beginning will save you much time further down the line. You could start with a basic loose leaf binder for each line of research and label it with the name of the line, for example, 'Williams family'. Within the binder you can separate out the information in a logical fashion, and keep in labelled sections such as 'census data' and 'certificates'. Invariably there will be overlaps between family lines but you can put photocopies in other relevant binders or put a note in to say where the related information is kept.

Kate's comment: In my household, I know not to leave pieces of paper lying about, as I cannot guarantee they will still be there when I return. I have lost count of the times that others in the family have taken 'phone messages and written them down on the nearest piece of paper – such as a newspaper extract detailing my great- grandfather's long distance running successes. I have even had what I would consider important documents used as handy paper for compiling shopping lists.

For those of you who are used to using computers, the idea of paper copies of information may seem somewhat outdated but there are advantages to keeping information in this form. Paper records bring together information gained from all sources, not just electronic ones. Many people find paper records much easier to read and review than screen-based ones.

Computers can make it very easy to order your information in logical form. You can set up a family history directory and have sub-directories within it which can mimic a paper filing system. You could have, for example, a sub-directory for 'Williams family history' and another for 'Jones family history'. Each sub-directory can be further divided into sections which suit your needs. Having your electronic records in one directory also helps easy transfer if you upgrade to a new pc and helps you back up your data.

Toni's tip: Keep stuff that you can't fit in anywhere at present in a separate section for the time being. Further analysis or discoveries may help you place this

Using a family history database from the start is a good idea, as it will help you organise your work in a logical fashion by linking evidence to individual names.

"Now the filing system was sorted, James was able to make a start on his family history."

Trap 13. You don't have the right kit

Whatever you set out in life to do, you need to have the right kit to do it with, whether it is redecorating the hall or planting a vegetable bed. Occasionally something can be bodged to do the job but there are occasions when only the right thing will do. Take for example the canoeing and camping trip that Kate's family and friends went on. After setting off and paddling vigorously down the river for a good distance, tired and thirsty and miles from civilisation, it was decided to pull out of the water onto a sandy bank and brew everyone a welcome cup of tea. The person responsible for supplies triumphantly brought out his brand new super all- singing-all-dancing gas burner and gas bottle. Rummaging through his kit bag, however, he sadly announced that he'd forgotten to bring any matches to light it with.   The intrepid explorers had all seen survival programmes on the television, so a lively debate ensued about striking flints, gathering dried moss, harnessing the power of the sun through a magnifying glass and other methods of lighting fires. Unfortunately none of this expertise was required as the rather haphazard quartermaster had also omitted to bring milk, fresh water, and, best of all, tea.

Basic kit for family history research is fortunately something that most of us are likely to own in the first place. But if you want to get the most out of your research and produce professional looking results, then the following list of equipment should help. To buy all this 'up front' could be expensive

> **Kate's comment:** *If you were to buy everything we suggest it would cost a small fortune, but you will probably get what you need over a period of time rather than having it all to start with. On the plus side, you will now have a large list of ideas to give to people when you are asked what you want for Christmas or your birthday.*

A personal computer (PC)

This will need to meet the specifications for whichever family history database and other software you choose. It will also need to have a sufficiently large hard drive to enable you to store images, which use up a lot of memory. The number of images to be stored quickly builds up, with photographs and scanned copies of documents so it is good practice to get a PC with the largest capacity that you can afford or extend your existing hard drive.

A wide-screen monitor
This is useful for displaying more than one program, website or document side-by-side at the same time. For example, you can make transfer of information into your database easily, and also you can make comparisons of data from different sources without having to switch between views.

Printer
When you are at the stage where you need to print out a family tree, you will generally find it quite difficult to fit this onto a single sheet of A4 sized (normal business letter size) piece of paper. If you can get an A3 (double A4) printer then you will have fewer pieces of paper to stick together to make the whole family tree. A3 printers are more costly than A4 but worth it. Larger printers than this are available but these start to get very pricey and if you want to get your tree printed on a single sheet of paper, without the joins, then it may be more cost effective to have a specialist tree printer handle this for you.

Toni's tip: I find it useful to have a well stocked stationery cupboard. That way you stay organised and don't have to delay your research whilst you nip down to the shops for some more sticky tape or a postage stamp. Items I like to have in my cupboard include: paper for printing (including scrap paper for notes); ruler, pens, pencils, pencil sharpener, highlighter pens, rubber; stapler; sticky tape and glue stick; sticky note pads; paper slicer/guillotine; magnifying glass; postage stamps; computer memory sticks or re-writeable CDs/DVDs; spare binders or folders; lots of A4 see-through punched plastic wallets; calculator and lastly, spare batteries. If you have children in the house you might need a locking cupboard or you may find your carefully hoarded supplies gradually go missing!

Scanner

These are especially useful when relatives lend you items for your research but wish for them to be returned. There are combined printer/scanner/photocopier and fax machines on the market which can be cheaper than buying a printer and scanner separately and take up less room on your workspace. The photocopying facility can be particularly useful.

Digital camera

Many record offices now let you use your own digital camera for recording images, which saves you time and effort which you would otherwise have used in taking notes. It can also save you money as you don't have to pay for photocopies.

A family history database

There are many on the market to chose from. Family history magazines regularly have reviews of new software which can help you decide which one is for you, or you can look to see if there are any forthcoming family history trade shows in your area. These usually have stands run by the major software houses and this will give you a chance to compare and see which one you like. Ideally the software will enable you to: store data including notes about individuals and events (with good search facilities to enable you to find individuals and make links); produce a number of different style trees and reports; and enable you to store photographs and images relating to individuals. Most will give you the ability to save your data in GEDCOM format. This facility will enable you to exchange data with others that do not have the same software package as you but which also support the GEDCOM format. Be discriminating; you can pay a lot for software which comes bundled in an impressive box with other disks that you have absolutely no need for. You could consider those which offer a free subscription to a commercial family history site as they can be worth having.

A word processing package

This is useful for typing up your notes, writing to relatives, drawing up questionnaires and many other tasks. Many new computers have a word processing package included in the purchase price or you are probably using one already.

High speed Internet link
This will enable you to make the most of what is available on-line without the need to go and make a cup of tea every time you attempt to download an image.

Trap 14. You don't use your tools properly

Hands up all those readers who own an automatic washing machine and know how to use it! Probably most of readers will by now have a hand in the air. Just have a think, though. How many wash programmes does it have? Ten? Fifteen? Twenty? And how many different programmes do you use when you put the washing on? Chances are that you use no more than three of them. So why do washing machine manufacturers give you so many options? Well, there are two potential reasons. The first one is that they may incorporate these to make themselves look good. The second is that you are not sorting your washing types and selecting the most appropriate programme for your wash. Given that the amount of costly time and effort the manufacturers must put in to develop the sophisticated software and mechanics that allows for a multitude of temperatures, spin speeds and timings, it seems unlikely that they are doing this to make themselves look good and eat into their profitability. So it means that you are probably not using your washing machine to its best advantage.

Are you making best use of all the software that is out there? There are probably many functions on the family history software you are using that you are unaware of, simply because you haven't really looked for them or worked out what they are. It's a good idea to familiarise yourself with the tools that come with your software, particularly the chart and report functions, such as:

- adding your own backgrounds to your family tree (perhaps of something relevant to your family – maybe a cornfield for a family of farmers, or a gallows if you had a murderer)
- adding photographs to your tree
- how to alter the size and type of text to prevent your tree going over loads of pages, or maybe move boxes around to get the best fit on a page
- explore the different reporting styles that are available. But bear in mind that to print off all options can become really unwieldy and unnecessary as they are often different views of exactly the same data. So take some time to work out what will be best for you.

Another overlooked aspect when creating your family history is enhancing images. You can use image manipulation software to improve your scanned and imported documents and even save you money. You may already have a basic package which was included with your PC but it may not be equal to the task. If you have a commercial package or even one of the excellent freeware packages, this will allow you to achieve much more. Some of the more useful things you can do, particularly with downloaded census images and parish records, are:

- straighten an image so it sits square on a page;
- crop off the black around the edge of the image to save you a lot of ink and maximises how it fits on the page and therefore easier to read;
- crop off any part of the image not relevant to you;
- enhance faded writing to bring out the text so it can be easily read;
- use it to show the date of the census and the area; plus
- highlight the family you are interested in; and
- append notes that may help someone interpret the image.

Toni's tip: Look for free on-line tutorials for your software to help you make the most of what you have.

Other tools which are readily available could include optical character recognition software (OCR) which can allow you to capture text from hard copy printed documents which can then be incorporated into your own design. Similarly screen shot capture software, such as a snipping tool, can capture an image of the screen or selected parts thereof.

Kate's comment: I had been thinking for some time that I wanted to get screen shot capture software for my PC, not realising that I had it already as part of the standard set up. I just hadn't thoroughly explored what software I already had. Your computer might already have this software and you may not realise it, so take a moment to have a browse through your list of programs.

Tempting though it might be, however, you might not please your family too much if you use your newly acquired digital manipulation software to give Granny a handlebar moustache and monocle, or turn your great-uncles into pantomime dames. And it will be noticed if you airbrush out your wrinkles and give yourself a size 34GG bust, especially if you are a man.

Trap 15. You fail to be kind to yourself

If you are a follower of Darwin's theory of evolution then you won't be surprised that a new sub-species of human has been identified. Known as Homo sapiens 'genealogisticus', they are identified by their stooped, shuffling gait, their inability to use their neck muscles; widely spread bottoms; pallid skin colour; their squinting, watering eyes, solitary nature and an alarming tendency to get over-excited if someone shows them a family tree. Don't be worried, they are mostly harmless, they just got that way because they failed to give themselves a break from time to time.

"When genealogists party"

Hopefully you are not yet at the stage, but you may find that long periods of sitting at a desk, particularly if you are using a computer, can start to cause damage to your eyes and back. In addition prolonged bouts of keyboard use could result in a repetitive strain injury (RSI).

If you are going to spend a long time in your chair, get yourself a decent one. It helps if it has lumbar support and is fully adjustable. You should be able to sit up close to the desk, which should be large enough and have sufficient room for anything you are working on, plus materials and equipment you need at the time. Whilst we are not suggesting you feng shui your work area or align your desk along a ley line, it does help to have your computer screen positioned away from direct sunlight.

Prolonged use of a laptop is not ideal, and you are not doing yourself much of a favour if, for example, you attempt to type whilst balancing the laptop on the arm of the sofa, whilst having a cat sit on your lap.

Kate's comment: *Educationalists suggest that students study in short bursts then go and do something else for a few minutes, as concentration wanders for most people after around 20 minutes. This is sound advice for family historians as well, as it helps to keep the mind alert and receptive. It is all too easy to become engrossed in what you are doing and not to realise how tired you have become, as Toni found whilst recently researching some records at the National Archives. After three hours spent reading, without a break, she noticed that nearly everyone she was reading about had the surname Porter. Her concentration had lapsed and instead of reading the 'Surnames' column she was reading the 'Position Held' column in railway employee records.*

Good lighting is important when you are working. If you want to read images that were written in pencil some 200 years ago it helps to have the best possible illumination. Your general lighting should be bright and clear and it also helps to have a good desk lamp and a magnifying glass.

> **Toni's tip:** *Pain should not be a natural consequence of sitting at a desk and using a computer, so if you experience this, seek medical advice. Varying your tasks not only makes you more effective but lessens strain on the body. Take regular breaks away from your computer screen, and go out occasionally into the sunshine if you want to avoid rickets.*

Sitting too long can cause problems worse than pain. It is well known that people on long-haul flights can have problems with deep vein thrombosis as a result of being still for too long, but perhaps less well known is the fact that there has been deaths due to sitting at a computer screen for too long. A young man from Sheffield died from DVT after spending 15 hours playing a computer game without breaks. Heart attacks, sleep deprivation and malnutrition caused by over-long computer use have all been reported, although these are of course extreme examples. Most of us can fall into the trap of 'I will just look this up and then stop' but we don't actually stop for some time. Whilst it is unlikely that as a family historian you are going to give yourself serious illness through over-use of a computer, it is sensible to take regular breaks.

We would like to politely suggest that although it is a good idea to have a break every 20 minutes or so, it is less of a good idea for these breaks to always involve tea and cake, otherwise the chances are you will have to get a bigger chair in a few months time.

Trap 16. You don't record as you go along

There are things in this world that normal people would make some effort to avoid, such as illness, pain, large angry animals with big pointy teeth, and housework; and included in this category is the routine, humdrum business of recording your family history data. There is a temptation to leave a lot of what you do to memory but this has its dangers. Many of you who are reading this book have at some time decided that you will remember to pass on a verbal message to someone rather than go through the tedium of finding paper and pen on which to record said message. Something then crops up which takes your attention and 'hey presto', message forgotten. Someone who is well known to the authors once forgot to pass a message onto his father that a close friend of his had died, and by the time his father found out, he had missed the funeral. Leaving things to memory can have serious consequences.

> **Kate's comment:** Some while ago I stumbled on some evidence that one of my relatives had gone out to Australia on an assisted passage and had eventually become a sheep farmer. It is an interesting story and one which could no doubt be verified quite easily. I could perhaps discover some family still in Australia, but unfortunately I don't know who it was about or where I saw it. There is always the possibility that my mind is playing tricks with me and the story relates to a different family entirely. Asking around my family has drawn a blank so the mystery may never be solved.

Most family historians enjoy the process of researching, and get a real kick out of finding information, but consider the recording of such information into a database or file to be a tedious chore. But if you are not rigorous in your recording, before long, a backlog of information awaiting processing can build up and this can become daunting. The thought of tackling this issue can put you off the whole idea of family history research completely. Having a pile of paper which is silently 'nagging' you to do something with it is not something that motivates many of us and this then becomes a duty rather than a pleasure, and who wants a hobby that is not fun to do?

> **Toni's tips:** If you are undertaking internet research, keep your database open on your screen. As you discover relevant information you can enter it straight onto your database, or cut and paste any snippets into the appropriate notes section for the individual concerned.
>
> Include information on your sources with each individual item of data. You may need to know where you got it from at a later date.
>
> Most record offices allow laptops, so taking one with you to enter your data onto will save much time, but if you are writing out your notes in pencil, try to get them entered onto your database or copied up for your files as soon as possible after returning home.

If you don't record you can end up researching the same aspect more than once because your unreliable memory has allowed you to forget the first time you did it. In addition, there is always something so important or obvious within your family history that you are sure that you will never forget it, but time and the pressures of life are bound to get in the way and you do forget either the fact or where you got it from.

The benefits of having a computer database far outweigh the disadvantages. Most modern programs allow you not just to enter standard birth, death and marriage dates but also to produce family trees, and append documents and photographs. Most have some kind of 'notes' facility where you can capture personal information about each individual. These notes can be automatically incorporated into genealogical reports generated from the database. Without such a facility, where would you record facts such as those about a certain David Durford. On the 1851 census, aged 80 years, he is described as having an income provided by the French government and also that he is insane – although we are not saying the two facts are necessarily linked. How much more enjoyable than just having 'dry' birth, marriage and death dates.

Trap 17. You don't know enough about the subject

One of the best things about family history is that you don't have to know much about it in order to make a start on it. For many, it is not until you have got a long way into it that you realise how little you knew about anything. Doing your family history will not only turn you into an expert researcher, but will also give you an insight into the many different influences that impacted upon your ancestors' lives. Most people begin with very little knowledge, just a keen interest, and they learn as they go along using a trial and error approach to their research. Whilst there is nothing wrong with this approach, there are some basics which may help you.

Some people find it useful at the outset to develop their research skills by taking a college course. Local adult education colleges, Family History Societies, Libraries and Record Offices often run short sessions on how to start on your family history. These can be invaluable to both beginners and those who have made a start but then get stuck. Major subscription sites offer very useful on-line tutorials, often on specialist areas.

Of course, the problem with knowledge is that you don't know what you don't know until you need to know it! There is little point in drawing up a list of books to buy or places to visit until you are sure they are actually of relevance. The trick is to know how you can find out about things, rather than having an encyclopaedic knowledge of everything. For instance, you don't need to be a geographical expert, you just need to know how to access a decent set of maps.

Magazines help make you aware of what is out there. There are a number of very good genealogy magazines on the market and investing in a subscription to at least one is a good idea. These magazines don't just tell you how to go about your research, but have fascinating articles about many aspects of social and family history, such as workhouses, guilds, and occupations. They help you keep up to date with developments and give you hints and tips on where to look for information and get the most out of your research.

Another useful route to help can be Family History Society magazines and journals, which have interesting member-generated articles. These Society members can carry a great deal of expertise and may be able to help with queries.

Over time, your basic knowledge of history, particularly social history, will grow and give you clues as to why, for example, your ancestors stopped working on the land and became builders in London's East End. So if you discover that an ancestor in 1860 moves from being an agricultural labourer in Essex and becomes a night soil collector in Tower Hamlets, you will be able to cheerfully tell friends and relatives about the old family business. If you're wondering what a night soil collector did, well, let's just say that when London's sewage transport and processing system was built during Victoria's reign, night soil collectors were out of a job.

Toni's tip: Get to know your local library and make use of their on-line catalogues to find specialist family history related titles. For a very small charge you can use their inter-library loan service to order your selections. What is also useful is that libraries often have free access to commercial genealogy sites.

You will never know everything, there is always something new to learn, and that is a big part of the fun of this hobby. Most of us keep one step ahead of wherever our researches take us, by reading around the subject concerned. Toni has this example:

"Many years ago, when I started my family researches, I have to confess that I did not really know what a Merchant Seaman was. Many earlier generations of my family were sea-faring, and whilst I was aware of the term and that records existed regarding merchant seamen, I did not realise that was what my relatives were. As a result I had missed out on a whole chunk of fascinating information, so when I finally made the connection and started to read up about early merchant seamen, I found it to be a wholly engrossing and complex subject."

"As soon as I was armed with sufficient information on what a merchant seaman did and how and where the records were kept, I was able to find information that wildly exceeded my expectations. For example, I was able to discover that my great-great-great grandfather first went to sea at eight years of age. I found out the names of the ships he had sailed on and the exotic ports he had visited. He had red hair and blue eyes, as I do, but was only 4ft 11ins tall at the age of 16; at least he wouldn't have had to duck when below decks!"

Trap 18. You don't have a back up

A philosopher might once have said: There are three certainties in life. These are Death; Taxes and Data Loss. There is not a lot you can do to avoid the first certainty; you can employ an accountant whom you can pay a fortune to in order to slightly lessen the second certainty; but there is something you can do about the third certainty – back-up your data!

Anyone who has ever used a computer has at some stage experienced the frustration of having a vital document disappear into the ether. Whether caused by virus, burglary, fire or flood, power surge, computer 'crash', incompetence or just sheer bad luck, it is never pretty to witness a grown person attempting to beat their computer with a stick. Toni has experienced losing data:

"I have been in the position where I lost the database for an entire family line during the changeover from one computer to another. As it was a line I wasn't currently working on, I didn't notice it had gone until a long time after the old computer had been scrapped. The database contained details of around 500 family members and the time researching and recording it represented a large chunk of my life which of course I shall never get back. What this has taught me is that I should always ensure that I have made back up copies of all my data."

Backing up your data can be done at more than one level and to be safe you need to employ more than one method of doing so. Your first level is simply to make a second copy of your data and keep it on your computer. Some family history programs can be set to automatically keep an up to date back-up file every time you use it.

Toni's tip: *Any back up file you create needs a sensible name so that you remember it is the back up. You should also ensure that any further work is done on the original file and that you are not working in the back-up file.*

If you have a lot of files dedicated to your family history, then it is a good idea to keep them all in one folder. It is relatively easy to copy a whole folder rather than keep on backing up individual files. It must be borne in mind, however, that taking back ups onto your own PC has limitations, as if anything happens to that PC then both your original and back up documents may be lost.

Your next stage could be to save copies onto either a USB memory stick or CD. These have the advantage of being small and easily stored but can also be broken or mislaid, and in the case of CDs these need to be labelled for ease of identification.

You can get an external hard drive for full back-ups of all the data on your computer. This will allow you to easily save everything on your computer as long as you remember to do so regularly.

There are on-line services that will store back up copies of data files. Some of these are free, some are subscription services and some require a one-off fee to be paid. Usually they require you to use their software in order to upload your folders and files to the service, or you may need to know how to compress your files for storage.

Toni's tips for making back-ups:
I like to make a back-up copy of my family history database on my computer before I do complicated work such as importing and merging data files – if, for example, I am adding some research provided by someone else. If the merge goes wrong then I still have the original file preserved.

Get yourself firewall, anti-virus and spyware protection. You can pay for this but there are free alternatives available on the Internet for downloading. It is important that these protection programs are updated regularly to take account of new threats.

Whichever method you elect to use, you should always check that the back up has indeed worked. Your mantra should be – back up, back up and back up again! You are guaranteed that when you need your computer the most, then that is when it is most likely to let you down.

Kate's comment: If you think it was a chore to record your findings the first time around, imagine just what a pain in the butt it is going to be to repeat the exercise. If you have to re-create it, it is probably not going to be as comprehensive as the first time around as your enthusiasm will have dramatically lessened. The amount of time you have spent on your data gathering is precious so it makes sense to spend a few minutes here and there making sure your information will not be lost.

So far we have only considered electronic data but of course you are likely to have some data in paper form, which is also beset with problems. Notwithstanding the dangers of disasters such as floods, lightning strike, tornadoes and fire; paper nowadays is made from wood pulp which is acidic and has a relatively short shelf life before it starts to weaken, yellow and eventually crumble to dust. Even the inks and boxes you use to store your paperwork in are likely to be acidic and make the situation worse. So even if you store your paperwork in something equivalent to Fort Knox, eventually it will deteriorate beyond use. This compares with older methods of recording information, such as ink on linen or parchment, which is naturally acid-free and can last for hundreds of years. It may, however, not be wholly practical to slaughter several flocks of sheep to provide sufficient parchment for your Smith one-name study.

Some consideration to your method of storing documents may be needed, especially those which you have obtained as a result of a journey, perhaps to a record office, or have had to send off for and pay for. Many companies dealing in supplies for family history research offer acid-free materials such as polypropylene wallets, paper, glues, tapes and inks which if used will help to prolong the life of your documents. Also consider copying important documents and lodging them at a separate location to your own. You might want to keep items in a fireproof filing cabinet but be aware that these are expensive and give only limited protection.

Toni's tip: As you print papers for your file or get new certificates, etc, take a copy for a second file. Store this together with any back-up computer data with another family member. As well as providing a valuable safe store, a second folder can be passed around to others in the family who may be interested in your research.

"Are you absolutely sure you need to look at Uncle Stephen's birth certificate?"

Trap 19. If you don't ask, you don't get

It is possible that all around the world, there are relatives of yours, wilfully (although not literally) sitting on piles of important documents which would be of immense value to you if only you could get your hands on them. It may well be the only reason you haven't been able to get hold of these documents is simply that you haven't asked for them. In fairness, even if you do ask to see any papers relating to family history, your family may not realise how useful some things may be. For example, old letters, medals, diaries, assurance documents, family bibles, notebooks and address books can all reveal information or hints to help the family historian but it might not occur to your relatives they are useful unless you ask specifically for them. Of course it goes without saying that anything you get this way you need to copy and return. If your family are not prepared to let you have items of interest now, you can always be cheeky and ask if they would bequeath them to you.

Toni's tip: Ask to borrow all family photographs, certificates and other interesting documents and either photocopy them or scan them into your computer for a more permanent record. That way, if anyone in the family does decide to destroy or get rid of important information, at least you have a copy. You could even offer to be the family 'Archivist', that is, hold onto all the family documentation. That way you can ensure it never gets lost or destroyed.

Kate's comment: You may well find that someone distantly related is also researching the same line as you or you may find a tree published on-line. Don't be afraid to contact the tree owners as you might strike lucky. I myself found a very distant relative who had a photograph of my great-great-grandparents. If I hadn't have asked him about the connection, I would never have seen what they had looked like.

But help can be obtained from other sources. Take this example from Toni:

"I like to carry out periodic surname searches on the Internet for names I am interested in, and whilst doing so I came upon a reference I had not seen before. It was within a legal document held in an archive, and clearly related to one of my ancestors. In order to look at this document I would have had to sign up for an expensive copying subscription service. However, I was able to establish to which set of records it referred and look around to see whether they were available elsewhere.

"I was pleased to discover that a further set of these records was located in a university library. I contacted the librarian at that university and asked if they were able to provide a copy and what the cost would be.

"The librarian responded quickly and helpfully. To my surprise, she undertook to scan and email me a copy of the required record free of charge. I was delighted to receive the document in question and it gave me some very interesting information about an early ancestor, which didn't cost me a penny."

> *Toni's tip:* You might feel a bit hesitant about asking for something – if this is the case, just think of the SAS motto – Who Dares, Wins!

Trap 20. You duplicate someone's research

Before you embark upon your voyage of discovery it's a good idea to check whether anyone else in the family has carried out any research. Imagine if you excitedly present the results of your endeavours to the family, only to be met with the news that it had all been done before. Much of the thrill of family history research is in the 'chase' and it can be very disappointing to find out that someone had got there first.

> *Toni's tip:* If you are serious about your family history you will want to check other's research thoroughly. Even if it is accurate there will probably be scope to add to it.

Bear in mind that other people's research may be far less diligent than your own, and wrong assumptions may have been made – for example, if there is more than one person with the same name it is possible that the wrong line may be followed. Of course, if the research is fairly old then it probably took your relative years of travelling to various archives to collect all the information they have; a feat nowadays easily accomplished in a much shorter period using Internet resources. This gives you the opportunity to flesh out or add to the research, particularly when you consider the developments in on-line indexes and records that allow you to find out even more about the lives of your ancestors. You will also be able to add newer generations to the family tree as family history should be a living, breathing entity. Your role could be to keep it up to date to ensure it reflects the latest additions to your tribe!

Toni's tip: Put the word out around your family that you are intending to start doing your family history and ask if anyone else has started this before. If you do find that someone else has already published a tree on-line which contains members of your family, check it out before treating it as fact.

The above assumes that your relative who has carried out the research is prepared to let you have a look through their work. This is not always the case, some researchers are very possessive about what they have done and will not under any circumstances reveal their findings until they feel themselves ready to do so – which may be never. This can be very frustrating, especially if other family members have already passed on photographs, certificates, letters and so on, and these are being hoarded by the person in question. If gentle persuasion doesn't work, then you will just have to grit your teeth and get on as best you can without them.

Trap 21. You try to follow more than one line at a time

There is a tale about the origins of the game of chess. The inventor took his new game to the Emperor, who was so impressed that he asked the inventor to name his reward. Simple, said the inventor. Just give me a grain of rice for the first square, then two for the second, four for the third and so on until you reach the last square. The Emperor gave instructions to his treasury for this to be carried out. Rather embarrassedly, the treasury minister came back after a while to explain that it would take many years to grow sufficient rice to fulfil this reward. Now imagine if you related this story to tracing your ancestors. You are one, you have two parents, four grandparents, eight great-grandparents, sixteen great-great grandparents, and by the time you get to 20 generations back (if you could find them all) you are talking 1,048,576 direct ancestors. In reality, you would find that because of intermarriage between families there is likely to be fewer people than that, but even if we assume half a million ancestors, then that is a mighty big family tree, and that is without including aunts, uncles, siblings, cousins and so on.

It is very easy to get carried away and try to follow each and every line. If you are haphazard in your approach, rather than being systematic, then you run the risk of getting muddled and not actually doing each line properly. Certainly you are less likely to find details and stories about every family; all you will be doing is collecting names and dates.

Each line researched generates its own paper trail and if you try to do everything at once then the result is bound to be chaos, no matter how ordered you think you are. The best way to proceed is to choose one line and go with that one until you have exhausted all immediate possibilities.

> **Kate's comment:** *Many people start with their surname but you might have a particular reason to follow a different line at the outset. If your surname is extremely common, why not start off by researching another, less common name, e.g. Your mother's or grandmother's maiden surname. An unusual name is much easier to trace and as your experience grows you can then move onto your own surname.*

Picking which surname to follow is a bit like trying to select one from your favourite chocolate selection box, as in the outset they all look tempting. You might fancy the hazelnut praline, the champagne truffle and the strawberry cream but to eat them at the same time might not be the best flavour combination! So too, if you follow more than one line at a time you might not be getting the best possible results from either line. We are not trying to suggest you stick with researching one line – unless you want to carry out a one-name study – rather, do them one at a time and try not to get distracted onto another line just because at the outset it looks more interesting.

Toni's tip: *If you are going to research more than one line at a time, be careful to keep all your information in separate files to avoid confusion. I like to keep a summary reminder sheet at the front of each file so that I can keep track of where I am with any particular line.*

You could be tempted away from your line as you go along, because something is discovered that looks interesting. When Kate was looking at a family history for a friend, it was discovered that this friend was directly descended from a fairly well-known 19th century watercolour artist. This was quite exciting as her friend is a sculptress and it was fun to show that art is 'in her blood.' However, it was also discovered that her watercolour artist ancestor was himself descended from a notable 18th century oil painter, but through a female line, not the direct male line. The temptation was to run away with researching the 18th century ancestor, which can be done in due course, but it would have taken her away from finding out all she could on her direct line.

Of course, the beauty of family history is that if you come to a stop on one line, you can put it to one side for later and there is always another line available to take its place.

WHAT'S IN A NAME?

Name-related problems and challenges

"Well, we named them after our favourite drinks. I named the girls, Sherry, Brandy and Chardonnay and Gary did our son, Special Brew."

Trap 22. Your relatives go by different given names

Sometimes you wonder why on earth anyone bothers to name their child at birth. Many of us go by names that we have acquired, to the extent that others may not even know your real name. Some are derivatives, e.g. 'Del' for Derek and some are common alternatives, such as 'Jack' for 'John' or some relate to the surname, e.g. 'Smudge' if your surname is Smith. This often means that when you are looking for someone in the indexes, you cannot find them with the name you know them by. The reasons for the change are many.

A common occurrence is where middle names are used in place of first names. One reason for this is where a child is named after their mother or father. So if you have two people named the same in a family then it can get confusing on a practical level and so the child's middle name is used in preference to his/her proper name. Toni has a variation on this – her father is called Tony, and so to ensure that each one knew who was being talked to, they became 'Big Tone' and 'Little Tone' and these names are still used to this day.

Another reason is that some people actively dislike their first name and will adopt the second name in preference to the first. Half of Kate's great-aunts and great-uncles have done this – looking for a birth date for a 'Frederick' has been a bit difficult when he actually is a 'Percy.' This is even more difficult if you are dealing with a frequently occurring surname. A wonderful example of an individual not liking his given name is the case of Napoleon John Moxhay, born in the 1850's. What on earth possessed his parents to give him the name of Napoleon will never be known, but understandably as soon as he was old enough to do something about it he went by his middle name, and so 'John' is how his descendants would have known him.

Toni's tip: *Always ask your relatives if they are aware of any other names that someone in the family may have. Even if the first name is correct, sometimes a middle name can help identify someone on a census or similar if there is a choice between more than one candidate.*

Another type of adopted name is where there is either a shortened version of the original name or a nickname that sticks to such an extent that no-one knows the individual's real name. A less obvious contraction of a first name was that of Vera, who after a tortuous search was discovered to be a Veronica. In Kate's family, there was an aunt called Raidie. When you are younger, you don't question names and they become so familiar you don't really think anything of them. When Kate started her family history, she was surprised and delighted to find that Raidie was so called because she was actually born right in the middle of a First World War air raid! Her real name was Gwendoline. As a result of this, because it was known where and when she was born the actual details of the air raid could be investigated.

Trap 23. You have fixed views about your surname

Contrary to popular belief, Samuel Johnson did not write the first English dictionary. However, he did publish, in 1755, what was held to be the first reliable dictionary which not only gave word definitions but also gave spellings for each word. Prior to Johnson, spelling was a creative process but now we have the situation where, for example, Radio 4 listeners would be spluttering into their morning porridge at the thought of the text shorthand used by mobile phone owners becoming accepted into general use. Grown men and women have been seen foaming at the mouth when presented with the spelling 'sox' instead of the BBC-approved 'socks'. Yet any language in use is by definition a living language and subject to change at short notice. The English language has arrived at its present state with influences from Latin, French, German, Greek, and even Chinese and Bengali, so with all these diverse influences it is not surprising how hard it is to arrive at standardised spellings either through common sense or phonetic rules.

But attempts to tame the variable and interesting ways of spelling ordinary words have had little effect on surnames over the last few hundred years. For a lot of the time, people were not particularly bothered how their name was spelt: even Shakespeare was known to spell his name in two different ways on the same document! Nowadays we aren't so relaxed about how our name is spelt; in fact, we can get quite annoyed when someone gets it wrong.

Toni has been blessed with a fairly unusual maiden name:

"My maiden name was Acott, which no one ever spelt correctly. I was forever correcting people, as I was often presented with one of these: Alcock, Allcock, Aucock, Apricot (Kate likes that one), or Haycock. Colleagues and friends no doubt got used to hearing me spelling it out: 'No, it's A - C – O – T – T, that's it, Acott'.

"Naturally I assumed that my surname had always been Acott. Imagine my surprise that when I researched the Acott line, my forebears had indeed been called Alcock, Allcock, Aucock and many other things beside, although unfortunately never Apricot. This variation was in part explained by a note in the Parish Registers by the Vicar of Brenchley, Kent, in 1816. When recording a baptism that he had just carried out, the Vicar put a note in the register that said: *'This name has been spelt by me here ACCOTT owing to the ignorance of the parents who could not read or write. I have reason to think that the name ought to be written ALCOCK.'* "

"His name is 'Allcock' but I understand it's a corruption of 'Allsock'."

Kate's comment: *Even a name that you would think was fairly straightforward, like Broad, manages to generate some variations. I never expected my married name of Broad to give people difficulties but I often find I have to confirm the spelling. I have been variously referred to as Board, Bored, Broard, Brod and even on one occasion, Beard.*

For many years, it was a minority of people who could actually read and write so entries made into official documents were most frequently scribed by the local Vicar or clerk. It is not surprising then that surname spelling variations occur when you take into account the levels of illiteracy, the effects of regional accents on the unwary or just the favoured spelling by the person making the entry. For example, the name Martin could be written as Martyn or Marten; similarly the Scots 'McLauren' could be Maclaurin, Maclauren, or McLaurin. The dropped 'H' of a London accent could easily cause misunderstanding of a surname like 'Hayden' and coupled with an ignorance of the name, it could be recorded as 'Aiden'. Such an important change to the spelling could cause immense difficulties when trying to follow the line back.

We should not be too hard on the poor old scribes, they were doing their best in difficult circumstances. When you consider the vagaries of the English language which can bring you surnames such as 'Cholmondeley' that is in fact pronounced 'Chumley' and, even more bizarrely, 'Featherstonehaugh,' which is pronounced 'Fanshaw', we should be more surprised when the scribes get it right! What we should not be is too rigid in our views about our own surname or the name we are following. We should expect it to change, and not be taken aback when it does. For a long time, consistent spelling was not a concept recognised by even the learned and in our experience the spelling of English surnames did not really start to settle down until around the mid-19th century, when literacy levels were starting to rise generally. Certainly when researching your family history, bear in mind that whatever spelling variants you have come across in your own lifetime, these are at some time in the past likely to have occurred, and plus some you never even imagined! Our favourite name change story, however, involves Toni's married surname, Neobard:

> "I needed to order a brochure from the Irish Tourist Board via the telephone. I had to leave a message on an answering machine. Knowing that the name Neobard frequently causes confusion I was very careful to spell it out clearly and succinctly, using the Police Phonetic Alphabet - N for November, E for Echo, O for Oscar, and so on. I was then delighted to receive my brochure through the post, addressed to Mrs N. E. O'Bard."

Trap 24. Believing the surname dictionary is correct

There we were, we British peasants, happy in our simple lives of turnip growing and dung shifting; we'd seen off the Romans long before and now were loyal to our King Harold, and answering to names like Egbert and Rufus. Then suddenly in 1066 along came those pesky Normans, who duffed-up our rightful leader and imposed their

William as king. But what else did they do for us? Well, they got the feudal system well and truly set up and on the way encouraged us all to have surnames. Mind you, it took about 300 years for the concept of hereditary surnames to become truly established.

If you don't already have a surname system in operation, then what can you use? It is widely acknowledged that there are four main ways in which people acquired surnames, which are:

- Occupation. These include names such as Cooper, Baker or Fletcher (an arrow feather maker, if you are wondering)
- Nicknames. Examples would be Redhead or Sheepshanks
- Patronymics. This is where a name is derived from a relationship, e.g. the son of a man called William may be known as Williamson.
- Place names, either somewhere you live or somewhere you own.

Surname dictionaries sell well. If you search on a major on-line bookseller you will get over 100 hits because people are interested in their names and like to know what they mean, or feel that their surname gives them some indication of their origins. Some surnames could be indicative of people's roots, say, if their surname is that of a place. For example, if your surname is Beverley then it is quite possible that your family, at least on the male line, has at some stage lived in Beverley, East Yorkshire and has taken the name of the place as the surname. But surname dictionaries are of limited use as they are written by language experts, not genealogists.

The better and more accurate surname dictionaries concentrate on the earliest form of the name and show where the earliest examples of people with that surname occur. But unfortunately many surname dictionaries give an explanation of a name which has just been compiled with unsubstantiated guesses. They will often look at just the modern version of the name and not take into account how it was in the past. It is also quite difficult to find agreement between the various dictionaries as to the meaning and history of the same name.

As we've already mentioned, Acott, Toni's maiden name, has had many variations over the years; 150 years ago it was Alcock, in the 16th century it was Aucock. One surname dictionary states the name Acott is derived from Glasscock while the name Alcock is derived from 'Son of Allen' and doesn't mention Aucock at all. So by implication they are unrelated surnames but as Toni's family have gone under all these surnames this is obviously not the case. It may well be that other people with the surname Acott have arrived at that name via Glasscock and maybe there are Alcocks who are descended from an Allen family.

Unusual surnames must present problems to dictionary compilers. The name 'Neobard' does not often appear in any modern surname dictionaries. It does, however, appear in one dated 1903 and gives the definition of Neobard as deriving from Anglo-Saxon, and is a corruption of 'Nithbeorht'. The dictionary gives a translation of this as 'Bright Need', which doesn't seem to make much sense. It is also wrong, as on tracing the name Neobard back, between 1700 – 1850 the name is spelt and pronounced 'Nebbard' and before that it was usually spelt 'Nevard', which does not sound even remotely like 'Nithbeorht'.

Toni's tip: Treat surname dictionaries with common sense. It is often very difficult for us to trace our own names back very far, so it would be completely impossible for dictionary compilers to trace every instance of a name back to its origins. In addition, the same name may arise from completely different sources in different geographical locations so as a guide to your origins they are of limited value.

On the other hand, you may be pleased that your surname isn't derived from your place of origin, especially if you came from villages such as Wetwang; Bonkle; Tiddleywink; Nempnet Thrubwell or even Llanfairpwllgwyngyllgogerychwyrndrobwllllantysiliogogogoch.

Trap 25. Being proud of the family crest

As individuals who take on commissions to trace people's family history, we always get a bit concerned when the client proudly announces that they have a family crest, because the chances are that they are in for a disappointment. People misunderstand the term 'family crest'. A crest is the description given to just one part of a coat of arms. A coat of arms was the traditional decorations originally used during the Middle Ages in tournaments to identify the contestants. They were displayed on the bearer's shields. This made the job of sports commentator much easier when trying to describe the outcome

"Err, the one with the pointy helmet has just been knocked off his horse – the crowd thinks it's all over – oh his heads been cut off – it is now."

of a jousting match! Any problems with identifying who was who could be referred to the heralds, whose extensive knowledge of the arms held by knights and their descendants brought about the beginnings of Heraldry.

It is incorrect to assume that the right to bear a coat of arms is linked to a particular surname as the right is either granted or inherited through the legitimate male line. Just because you have the same surname as the original owner, this doesn't mean you have the right to those arms – you may not be related to the original bearer at all, who would have been part of the nobility of the day. Unless you can show descent from nobility your chances of being a legitimate bearer of arms are very small indeed.

Heraldry in the United Kingdom is very tightly controlled. The bodies in charge of this are the College of Arms, who cover England, Wales, Northern Ireland and the Commonwealth; in Scotland, the Court of the Lord Lyon King of Arms fulfils this function. Other countries may allow you to design and register your own coat of arms, either based around one belonging to someone with the same surname as yourself or even allowing you to draw up your own from scratch.

Toni's tip: If you suspect that you are one of the privileged few who are entitled to bear arms, then you would need to approach the College of Arms for a search of their very extensive records to confirm whether or not you are entitled. The College of Arms make a charge for this service.

However, if money is no object, it is quite possible to purchase your own entitlement to arms, as a number of high profile celebrities have done. The process is quite straightforward. You would need to send your Curriculum Vitae to the College of Arms. They have no specific criteria for eligibility to arms but will take into account such things as *"awards or honours from the Crown, civil or military commissions, university degrees, professional qualifications, public and charitable services, and eminence or good standing in national or local life"*.

If the College of Arms gives you favourable feedback, then a petition will be drawn up for your signature, you will be required to pay a fee (in 2012 this stood at £4,725), and your arms will then be drawn up, incorporating any ideas you might have as to what should represent you. As coats of arms usually reflect in some manner the personality or interests of the bearer, then you can have something that shows, say, your hobbies or occupation. Should you happen to work in the City of London and breed pigs as a hobby, then you could perhaps suggest having a sow rampant upon a bowler hat, although we cannot guarantee the College of Arms would approve of that.

Companies exist who will attempt to sell you English titles, which can cost from around £200 to £1000, sometimes promising land as part of the package. They have particularly good sales in the United States of America, but if you are thinking of buying yourself a Baronetcy or Knighthood, this is probably not the best way to go about it, as the sale of British titles was made illegal by the Honours (Prevention of Abuses) Act of 1925.

A quick trawl through the Internet will reveal a host of companies who are happy to sell you your 'family crest' emblazoned on t-shirts, mugs, key rings, Christmas ornaments, teddy bears, jigsaw puzzles or even cheese boards but their worth in genealogical terms is practically zero. Take a surname such as Mitchell, which is a common name in most parts of the United Kingdom. You can easily buy goods emblazoned with the Mitchell family crest but the companies that sell these cannot possibly investigate each buyer's heraldic entitlement, so whilst not strictly a scam, they can be misleading. No doubt at one time there was a good Sir Mitchell, or similar, who proudly sat astride his noble steed, armed and armoured, ready to do battle. You may of course be directly descended from good Sir Mitchell but you may equally well be descended from an unrelated Mitchell whose job it was to clear up the horse droppings after the tournament had ended. Unsurprisingly, the Mitchell coat of arms does not have a shovel on it.

Teap 26. You trust that old family tree

Toni's sister-in-law, Sue, possesses a very important sounding double-barrelled surname: Harrison-Chinn. It is the sort of surname that you can imagine being attached to a high ranking military officer, General Harrison-Chinn, or in the Church of England: Archbishop Harrison-Chinn. Certainly Sue always felt she was of noble extraction, and the magnificent family tree she has inherited shows her lineage stretching back through many notable and noble families all the way back to King Edward the Third, via a son of John of Gaunt. The tree is beautifully presented, with many representations of the various Arms held by individual members and branches of the tree. Undoubtedly it is a Work of Art. It is also undoubtedly a Work of Fiction.

It starts off promisingly. Edward III did have a son, John of Gaunt. However, the family in question is shown as descending from John of Gaunt via a son who never existed in any documentation. Additionally, titles bestowed upon his descendants do not seem to exist or if they do, they seem to relate to someone else. Dates given are incorrect and nor do any recorded marriages fit with those of the true descendants of John of Gaunt. There is a letter attached to the tree, supposedly from the College of Arms, that indirectly authenticates some of the names on the tree but the information contained in the letter does not stand scrutiny, and it is probable that this is also a fake.

So where did this tree come from? The original owner was Sue's grandfather, Frederick. Frederick appears to have had somewhat humble origins but was obviously talented and successful, having achieved financial success during his lifetime, although he was apparently not particularly well-liked as a person. He was known to have adopted airs and graces which fell away once he had a glass or two of port. Being a bit of a social climber, it is very likely that he was responsible for the production of the family tree. For example, the tree clearly shows that the name Harrison-Chinn occurred when two great families, the Harrisons and the Chinns, intermarried four generations previously. However, a browse through the London Gazette of 1918 shows that Frederick changed his name by Deed Poll from plain old Chinn to the double-barrelled one. By changing his name and appearing to demonstrate that he was from 'good families' he would have been able to move in circles that may have otherwise been denied him.

Sue is by no means unique in possessing a falsified family tree. Faking pedigrees is something that can be shown to have happened from Elizabethan times, and may have occurred even earlier than that. The Victorians were frequent offenders and these older forgeries are now often incorrectly treated as fact.

Not all false pedigrees were necessarily constructed to improve the social standing of the owner. Many mistakes were made through ignorance, supposition or transcription error. This problem has worsened in recent years with many false pedigrees being published on the Internet.

There are people who claim that they can trace their family trees to Jesus, and the College of Arms possess a pedigree that link the British royal family, via King David and Adam and Eve, directly to God. A recent survey revealed that 62% of Britons believe that they are related to royalty. Considering the number of offspring that royalty had in the past, whether legitimate or illegitimate, there is probably a good chance that you are, distantly, linked to a member of the royal family. Genetic scientists have shown that European DNA is the least diverse amongst all the races of the world, and bearing in mind the theory that the first 'colonists' to arrive in Europe from Africa some 40 – 50,000 years ago only numbered around 100, then there is every chance all people of European descent are related to each other!

Toni's tip: Just because you are now 'ordinary' there is no reason to suppose that your ancestors were, too. Inheritances can be watered down over time, bad marriages made or fortunes lost through ill-advised investments or gambling. If you are fortunate to be able to make a link with nobility you will have what is called a 'gateway ancestor'. Most noble lines are well documented, and you will therefore have access to a network of published pedigrees that can take you back much further than those people with purely humble origins can hope for.

Trap 27. Your family changed their surname

It's probably true to say that if you were given the name Emma you would probably be quite satisfied with that. If, however, you happened to be the Emma Turd (yes, really!) who was born in Hartley Wintney in 1877, then you might have been quite keen to dump the surname (if you pardon the phrase) as quickly as you could. I bet Emma couldn't wait to get married, although probably not to Mr William Shit of Wisconsin (and he was real, too!). Or at the very least not make it a double-barrelled surname.

People change their surnames for a variety of reasons, not just because their surname is, literally, Shit. Take, for instance, Mr Harrison-Chinn, who changed his for status reasons. No doubt it helped him considerably in his chosen career and lifestyle. Some people may fall out with their family and change surname to avoid being associated with their relatives. Others may wish to distance themselves from a famous or infamous name, such as the decline in popularity of the name 'Adolf' after 1945.

Kate's comment: Embarrassment over your name is a valid reason for wanting change, as Mr & Mrs Curtin's daughter, Annette, or Mr and Mrs King's son Lee, may well want to testify to. My husband managed to talk me out of my hormone-fuelled wish to call our firstborn son 'Norfolk' Broad, thankfully!

It was a fairly common practice for immigrant people to Anglicise their names when settling into the United Kingdom or other English speaking parts of the world. They would have done this to avoid discrimination, to fit better into the culture, or to make it easier for others to pronounce and spell their surname. Many US families have stories that their family surname was changed on arrival at Ellis Island because of communication or translation problems. In reality this is unlikely to be the case as the immigration officials had rules that prevented them changing identifying information for any immigrant unless specifically requested to do so by him or her. However, many people did change their surnames once settled in their new country.

> **Toni's tip:** *If you think your ancestors may have been of foreign extraction, their new surname can often be a clue to their old name, for instance, people often adopted the nearest sounding name to their own, so the Schmidt family from Germany, became Smith and their friends, the Braun family, became Brown.*

It is worthwhile noting, however, that in 1916, all 'enemy aliens' living in the United Kingdom were forbidden to change their names. This ban was extended to all foreigners in Britain in 1919 and this restriction continued until 1971. The only way to change your name in that period was if a new name could be assumed by Royal licence; or by special permission of the Home Secretary; or when a woman took her husband's name on marriage. With the first two of these options, the name change had to be advertised in the Gazettes.

> **Toni's tip:** *Names and information about foreigners coming to live in Britain during the past six hundred years can be obtained from various records in The National Archives.*

Women could change their surname to hide the fact that they were not married to the person they were living with. Because divorce was a rare and unusual occurrence and the emphasis was on marriage for life, anyone attempting a divorce had to have a good reason for doing so. Often if a woman obtained a divorce it would be at the cost of her home, children and financial support and so was not undertaken lightly. Any dowry she brought into the marriage would remain in possession of the husband, regardless of who was at fault. A woman without any tangible means of support was in a very difficult situation indeed. As a result, many marriages did fall apart but the respective individuals went to live with another partner. The woman would take the name of the new partner even though they were not married, as this would avoid gossip and speculation about them 'living in sin'. Marriage was not an option as the penalties for bigamy were severe, although a belated wedding often took place after the original spouse died. Children of the first union would use the surname of the new partner, possibly without being aware that it was not their original surname.

There is not a lot you can do, unfortunately, if you had an ancestor who was somewhat on the dodgy side, who adopted different surnames in a bid to outwit the forces of law or the bailiffs. Unsurprisingly, people who made name changes for this kind of purpose were not going to leave a trail (if they could possibly avoid it) in order to allow the police to track them down. This of course means that a future family historian is equally unable to find them. Some habitual criminals, along with their aliases, are indexed at the National Archives at Kew but these are in a minority.

Tracing people who have changed their name is not straightforward. This is because under English common law, a person may take a new surname, perfectly legally, without drawing up any formal record, provided that such action is not undertaken for the purpose of fraud or avoidance of obligation. Any methods of recording name changes were mostly voluntary, such as by use of a Deed Poll (a deed of change of name). The majority of people in the past would not have bothered with a Deed Poll as this would have to be drawn up by a solicitor who would charge a fee. Additionally, there is no central organisation within the United Kingdom which holds records of name changes. Nowadays, anyone who wants to change their name is fully entitled to, but if they wish to apply for a passport then they need evidence such as a Deed Poll.

Toni's tip: *If you believe your ancestor changed his surname, and if you were fortunate that he did so using a Deed Poll and enrolled the name change in the Close Rolls for safekeeping in the Supreme Court of Judicature, then you may be in with a chance of finding his original name. The Rolls remain for several years with the Supreme Court and then get passed onto the National Archives at Kew and searching through these can be a long drawn out process. You might also find evidence of a name change in either of the London, Belfast or Edinburgh Gazettes.*

There were other methods of making a change of surname such as by Royal Licence or private Act of Parliament, but these were unusual and also needed to be advertised in the appropriate Gazette or the Times newspaper.

The process of changing your surname is quite simple, perhaps too simple. The authors wonder what the parents of Mr Happy Spanners (middle name, Adjustable) think of his new name and possibly still refer to him by his birth name, Daniel. Similarly, how difficult it must be to get used to your offspring discarding their lovingly bestowed names and subsequently call themselves Jellyfish McSaveloy or General Ninja Ant?

Trap 28. Collecting every instance of your name

If you have an unusual surname, such as the unfortunately named Splatter, Strangle or Arse families (all of which are real surnames) then you may be tempted to collect every recorded incidence of that name. This is known as a one-name study, as opposed to the normal family history research that either seeks to find a person's ancestors or takes a person in history and seeks to find his/her descendants. This is something that is reasonably achievable if it is an unusual surname. Should your surname be Smith, however, then to collect every instance of the name would be a lifetime's work probably best suited to someone with an Obsessive Compulsive Disorder.

There are a few organisations dedicated to the art of one-name studies, the most well known being the Guild of One-Name Studies. This organisation will help its members set up a study by offering guidelines on how it should be done or assist with bringing people together who are already under way with a study of the same name. It also has an interest in other types of surname study, such DNA projects.

The most common reason for starting a one-name study is if someone has gone as far as they are able with their own ancestry and hit the proverbial 'brick wall'. By collecting all instances of their surname they hope that this will enable them to make links, for example, to follow a trail where one person has moved from one area to another. Often this kind of activity can be of great use to the family historian. However, for every connection you are able to make, another 20-odd snippets of information may be found that you are unable to link in.

"If you don't behave, I'll send you to the Bad Ass section over there."

More often it means that the person carrying out the one-name study becomes an expert on that surname, even when it is attached to a family that has absolutely no link with his/her own at all. If you do become involved in a one-name study and publish the results, you are likely to attract enquiries from people from all over the world. This of course can be very interesting as you get to communicate with people from all walks of life but there can be a down side to this. If you find yourself in the position of being the all-knowing expert on a name, you can get so many enquiries that you end up spending a huge amount of time writing replies and getting involved in sorting out other people's research at the expense of your own.

Kate's comment: Consider carefully how widely you publish the findings of your one-name study. Whilst family history researchers are traditionally very generous with their help and time, and we wouldn't want to discourage this, you have to decide whether you have the time available to dedicate to helping many others sort out their research. On the other hand, whilst it can be time-consuming helping other people, you may reap benefits from findings that others have made and will share with you.

One name studies in Britain are a little more straightforward to carry out than those in other countries. Records of British births, marriages and deaths are in the public domain and any individual can apply to see these records. Indexes to the registers are available on line. The story is not the same in all other countries, as many do not have indexes on-line, nor do they have one central depository for records; rather, they would be split by region, which could mean a hard slog and be time-consuming for the researcher.

Toni's tip: *If you have a reasonably unusual surname, it is worth looking to see if anyone is carrying out a one-name study of that name. This may result in a real boost to your researches, but the usual warnings apply – always treat others' research with a degree of scepticism as you don't know how thorough they have been.*

Of course, some names are far easier to follow than others and have relatively few recorded occurrences. The US Federal censuses taken during the 19th century detail a few names which do not crop up very often, for example, there were 430 incidences of the surname Bollock; 272 of Nipple, a very creditable 250 mentions of Bugger; Bum managed 119. There were 44 Tossers, but poor old Jerkoff only featured twice.

Trap 29. Adoption – surname research ends here?

Lots of people enjoy going to fancy dress parties and often have a costume of choice, relating to their interests or something in their background. Imagine if your name is Tom Sorensen, and your costume of choice is that of a Viking. Why? Because, obviously, Tom knows that with a surname like Sorensen, he has to originate from a Scandinavian country and therefore likes to wear his Viking costume to the supermarket at weekends.

When Tom eventually gets around to tracing his family history, he gets back to Henry Sorensen, born around 1820 in London. Hoping to find something on Henry's history, he finds the baptism entry in the records office. It states "Henry Sorensen, was baptised today, a foundling infant abandoned in Sorensen Street about 10 weeks old." Poor old Tom, he was hoping to find that Henry's father was Erik

Bloodaxe Sorensen from Denmark. Instead, he finds that Henry was named after the street he was found in. Not only are the chances of finding out details of Henry's parents very slim, but equally slim are the chances that he has Scandinavian roots.

It was very common for abandoned children to be given a name based on where they were found or the person finding them. A glance through parish records will give you real examples such as Rose Milton. Her christening was on 7th April 1837 at St Luke Old Street, Finsbury. The description given was that Rose was abandoned in a lodging house in Milton Street, and she was estimated to be about 7 weeks old. Another child found abandoned on the steps of St Gregory's & St Paul's Church, London, around the same period of time was baptised Paul Gregory.

Having an ancestor who was an abandoned child is most likely to be an insurmountable barrier to further research along that line. If the authorities of the day did not know who the parents were, then there is not a lot of hope that you will be able to discover them. Similarly, tracing children who were brought up by others is equally problematical. There was no legislation covering adoption until 1927. Prior to that date, all adoptions were either informal or arranged privately through an agency.

Where informal adoptions took place, the child would often be given the surname of the adopting parents and it is quite possible that the child themselves would not know of their adoption. Certainly no public records of the adoption would exist and so there is very little hope of knowing who the birth parents would have been. If the child was informally fostered then he or she might have kept their original surname. Should this be the case then it may be possible to trace their birth mother but in the case of illegitimacy, it would be very unlikely that the birth father would be located. Many children would have been adopted after being orphaned but a significant proportion would have been illegitimate and taken on by a family member or friend.

Some orphaned or abandoned children were looked after in a workhouse, foundling hospital or by Dr Barnardo's. If your relative falls into this category, then records of his/her admission and stay at the institution might be available, but often those records are incomplete or patchy and may not give you any details about the child's parentage.

In the early 18th century, there were an alarming number of

abandoned or orphaned children, particularly in parts of London, where the gin craze, aided by epidemics of typhus, dysentery, measles and influenza, was ensuring a steady supply of children in need of help. Such children were the responsibility of the parish so they were placed in the parish poorhouse or, after 1722, the workhouse. Childhood mortality was high; some research indicates that in parts of London, 74% of infants did not make it past age 5. This figure increased to 90% for those in the workhouse.

Clearly this situation could not be permitted to continue, so in 1739 the first Foundling Hospital was created by Royal Charter granted to Thomas Coram, a master of a trading vessel, for the "reception, maintenance, and education of exposed and deserted young children." The first two children to enter the premises in 1741 were named Thomas Coram and Eunice Coram, after the founder and his wife.

The popularity of leaving an unwanted child at the Foundling Hospital quickly grew, when eventually a situation arose where places were only available for one in five children brought in. At one stage a ballot was created so mothers bringing in their child had to draw a 'winning' ball from a bag in order for their child to be admitted. So in 1756 a resolution was passed in Parliament that receiving places should be set up around the country and funds provided for this. At the Foundling Hospital in London, a basket was hung outside the door so that people bringing in babies could place them in the basket and ring a bell to alert the officers in attendance. On the first day of this measure being put into place, no less than 117 babies were placed in the basket.

The Foundling Hospital Archives are held by London Metropolitan Archives. These records cover many elements of the children's lives and the activities of the Hospital and include the General Registers, Petitions, Baptism Registers, Inspection Books, Nursery Books and Apprenticeship Registers. Registers containing personal information about named individuals remain closed for 110 years. However former pupils of the Foundling Hospital and their relatives can request information from closed records by contacting the Coram charity.

The situation regarding abandoned, neglected or orphaned children had not been resolved by the time that Thomas Barnardo came to London in 1866 and saw for himself the numbers of poor, malnourished children forced to sleep on the streets. By 1870 he had set up his first home. His policy was to find foster homes for infants and younger children, with older girls being trained for domestic service and boys taught a trade. Many of the children were sent to Canada and Australia and other parts of the British Empire to start new lives.

The Barnardo's organisation took a photograph of every child taken into its care and so has a vast archive of images. If you think an ancestor of yours was a Barnardo's child, then for a modest fee their in-house archivist will carry out a search on your behalf.

For children adopted after 1927 a certificate of adoption was drawn up and this is held at the General Register Office. If you are the adopted person and you are over 18, you can apply for your adoption certificate. This will tell you the date of adoption and the court which undertook the necessary formalities, but will not tell you the names of your birth parents. You can then apply for your adoption details to be released to you. If you were adopted before 1975 you will have to undergo counselling before being allowed to have the records.

An adopted person's direct descendants can also apply for the adoption records to be released to them; however, this can only be done through a court application.

It should be noted that adoption papers cannot always tell you everything you need to know; for example, you may only get your mother's name and your place of birth, and if your birth mother's name is a common one then you may not be able to progress your researches any further back.

Watch this space, however. There are research programmes under-way that seek to develop techniques that will allow the police to work out surnames from DNA evidence alone. If genealogists can get hold of this technique then family history research will get a whole lot easier ....

Trap 30. Same surname, not necessarily connected
Jim and Beverley Hartford have gone off to Barbados for their annual holiday. After a few delicious rum punches, they get chatting to the nice couple from Cheshire who are at the next table. What a surprise! It turns out that they are also called Hartford and, amazingly, they come from the village of Hartford, in Cheshire. In fact, they believe that his family have lived there for hundreds of years and take their surname from the name of the village. It is not a very common surname so our Jim and Beverley immediately make the connection – that is where Jim must have originated from.

We have already established that some surnames can be derived from the place where the person with the surname is from but, of course, this is not necessarily a reliable indication of where your family originates. Jim and Beverley didn't know that there are also villages called Hartford in both Northumberland and Cambridgeshire – not to mention Hartford End in Essex, and their version of the surname could easily have derived from one of those places. The name Hartford itself may be a corruption of a different name and have no link to a place name at all. So having the same surname is not a reliable indication that your families are genetically linked, and Jim and Beverley may be disappointed to discover that they have not in fact discovered some distant cousins.

A lot of time can be wasted trying to make a connection where none exists. A very uncommon surname may possibly have its origins with one man. All men currently with that name may be his direct descendants and be able to be fitted onto the same family tree. However, the reality is that most surnames are not that uncommon and examples of each can be found in different areas and have differing derivations. A name like Johnson (likely derivation: son of John) appears throughout the UK and no doubt has its origins with many sons of many Johns.

Advances in genetic testing are beginning to establish where links can be made with surnames. The Y chromosome on human DNA is the bit that establishes maleness and is passed down from father to son. So there can be a simple link between surname and type of Y chromosome and theoretically all males bearing a particular surname descended from one man should show a link through their DNA. This of course has problems as it is often the case through second marriages, name changes, infidelity and adoption, that an individual bearing a surname does not have a genetic link to the person known as or recorded as his father.

Research carried out at the University of Leicester has demonstrated that men with the same surname have on average a 24% chance of sharing a common ancestor. This percentage increases to nearly 50% if the surname in question is an unusual one.

So if our friends Jim and Beverley want to find out if they are related to their new friends in Barbados, they need to get a male from each family to take a Y chromosome DNA test. Comparison of the results will give an indication of the likelihood of having an ancestor in common, with the more markers shown, the more accurate it will be. There are many genetic services that offer these tests. Most will also provide a database where your results can be posted for automatic matching against other people's results (or you can post results yourself to other databases). The matching service will usually estimate the number of generations back that there are to the nearest common ancestor.

"I'm sorry Mr Plantagenet you do not share any DNA with the royal family, however we think we know why you like bananas so much."

DNA testing has helped prove a theory which was formed between Toni and another experienced family historian, Carol Nubbert. They were convinced there was a link between the names Nubbert and Neobard, but could not prove this link through conventional paper-based researches, so they decided to give DNA testing a go.

Carol Nubbert had been researching the Nubbert name for 14 years, and carried out a one-name study. She had traced the family back to one Joseph Nubbert/Nubberd/Nubbard who died in December 1837 in Moulsham, Chelmsford, Essex. He was recorded as aged 70 at the time of his death making his birth around 1767, but then the trail went cold. So she contacted Toni after seeing her name on an on-line genealogical forum as part of her one-name study into the Neobard name. Carol wanted to know if Toni had any individuals called Joseph, born around 1767, who may have gone missing from the family tree. Toni did: a Joseph who was baptised in Eye, Suffolk in 1757. The date wasn't perfect but the possibility was there.

Carol suggested that DNA analysis might help prove a link. Both thought it worth a go, but accepted that the chances were slim - not only may there never have been a connection between the families, but it was possible that there could be illegitimacy on either line which would take the genes down another path. To carry out the analysis a Y-46 DNA test was carried out on the male lines: one from Toni's husband and the other from Carol's father.

Amazingly, when the results were back it was found that they matched. The ancestor in common was estimated as being 10 generations back – the generation of the 'missing' Joseph. So if you find yourself in a similar situation, then Y-chromosome DNA testing might be the solution for you!

THE MAN WHO NEVER WAS

Overcoming problems with BMD indexes and certificates

"I told them the Reverend Spooner wouldn't cope with the name Bertie Dugger."

Trap 31. Not understanding the registration process

It was December, 1852. Eli Hepplethwaite bade farewell to his wife, nursing their latest child, a boy, whilst the seven older children played or helped their mother with her duties. Wrapping himself up in his greatcoat, the snow swirling in the icy easterly wind, he began the long cold trudge down the valley from his hillside sheep farm towards the town. After three hours, soaked and frozen to the skin, he arrived and knocked at the Registrar's door. The Registrar's wife answered: no the Registrar wasn't there, he was down in Richmond on business for a couple of days. Eli turned around and began the three hour trek back to his farm. "I'll register t'boy another time," he thought, "when t'weather clears a bit." Of course, as it was Yorkshire, by the time the weather had cleared, he had forgotten.

Eli Hepplethwaite's great-great-great grandson now has a problem. He has found the birth records of all of Eli's children except for the one he wants – his direct ancestor. Registration of births, marriages and deaths was introduced on 1st July 1837 to England and Wales, to Scotland from 1st January 1855, and Ireland from 1st January 1864. It was in fact compulsory to register, but the wording on the legislation was confusing. Between 1837 and 1874 anyone failing to register an event would not have been prosecuted.

Eli's local Registrar was entitled to be away. Up to 1874, being a Registrar was considered a part time occupation, with most Registrars having a primary job such as being a butcher or a Poor Law Union official. Although the onus was on parents to register births, Registrars were paid piecemeal, that is, they received a sum for each registration entry they made, so they had an incentive to visit the house where someone had been born or died and make the registration entry. However, in Eli's Registrar's case, he may well have considered the remuneration unequal to the six-hour cross country visit to Eli's farm and he too would conveniently have forgotten about the new arrival.

Those Registrars who had responsibility for inner city slum areas may also have felt from time to time that the remuneration available did not adequately cover them for the risks involved in visiting areas where overcrowding and impoverished conditions often led to epidemics of scarlet fever, cholera and typhus. Of course, during an epidemic there would be a lot of deaths to register and understandably, any Registrar would have had doubts about entering the area. These slum areas, too, were where many new immigrants would end up; it would be unlikely that they were aware of their legal requirement to register events. If the Registrar was a reluctant visitor to the district then many births may not have been recorded.

Registration was brought about primarily to create legal documents that establish and protect the civil rights of the individual. A secondary purpose was to use the information gained from registration as a source of data which could be used to compile statistics about the population in general. Of course, civil registration provides a fantastic resource for genealogists and coupled with census returns, these records are the primary source of information on our forebears. Cross-referencing registration with census data enables us to establish and confirm each link in the family line. An understanding of the registration process will help you to avoid forking out for the wrong certificate.

From 1874, the legislation regarding civil registration was tightened up. The wording of the new legislation made clear that registration was compulsory and that penalties existed against those who did not register an event. From this time on, register offices were to have fixed hours of opening. A Superintendent Registrar had charge of a whole district and he could register births, marriages and deaths. A local Registrar could do just births and deaths. Regardless of which type of Registrar you were, you still had to have a place of business, although not necessarily a register office. Registrars came from all walks of life, and people with primary occupations such as carpentry or tailoring, could become a Registrar and work out of their primary business premises.

Central records of births, marriages and deaths for England and Wales are held by the General Register Office (now part of the Home Office – Identity & Passport Service); and regionally by the Superintendent Registrars for events that happened in their locality (District Register Offices). Nowadays, everything is computerised but in the past the General Register Office records were compiled from a quarterly return of birth and death registrations made by each District Registrar. Marriage returns were still submitted quarterly to the GRO but came from two sources. Those weddings which took place in a Church of England, Jewish or Quaker church were submitted by the clergymen concerned; but records of marriages which took place in a register office or in other churches were recorded and submitted by the District Registrar. These rules changed slightly over time to allow non-conformist churches such as Methodists to have an appointed person who would maintain an official marriage register instead of requiring the involvement of the District Registrar.

The GRO indexed them in alphabetical order of surnames, into quarterly lists which are dated when the registration took place, not when the event took place. In the case of marriages and deaths, the time difference between event and registration is usually minimal, but in the case of births, the law allows for a 42 day (6 week) registration period after the event.

This period of grace had the effect that if parents did not get around to registering a birth within the required six weeks then they would often give a false date of birth when registering so that they would not get into trouble with the law. This can mean that families celebrate a different birth date to that one shown on a birth certificate. It can also mean that when a family historian is looking for confirmation of a birth date, they may search the wrong quarter and not be able to find it.

Toni's tip: *If someone was born, say, at the end of March, registration may not take place until April and subsequently be shown on the April-May-June quarter for the year in question. A birth in December 1902 may well not appear until Jan-Feb-Mar 1903. So if you can't find a registration when you expect it, look in the next quarter.*

Registration districts can also complicate matters for the family historian. Registration districts were originally based around the boundaries of the Poor Law Union districts but have undergone numerous changes since then. Helpful information can be found on two free major genealogy web sites: GENUKI and FreeBMD.

Registration districts did and still do cover quite large areas and some geographical knowledge may be needed in order to track down your ancestor. For example, a baby born in Yaxley, in Suffolk, would appear in the lists under the Hartismere Registration District, which is even more confusing when Hartismere as a place doesn't really exist.

The registration entries are indexed, and it is these indexes that we use to identify the particular birth, marriage or death that we are interested in. The index details will not give you very much detail, only the name, date and district of registration. That may be enough, but if you want more information about your relative, or indeed confirm that it is your relative, you will need to order a copy of the registration certificate. Many people complain about having to shell out for these relatively expensive bits of paper, especially as they only want the details and do not really need a certified copy of the entry. However, a copy of the certificate has to be obtained, because in the wording of the 1836 Act for England and Wales it states that information will only be given out in the form of a certified copy of an entry in a register. Scottish and Irish records differ because of the wording of their later Acts. This means that you can get information you need for a smaller charge, rather than having to buy the certificate.

To obtain a certificate, you can ask for the GRO to search out your relative for you, which they will do, but it will take longer. If you give them details from the index it will speed up the process.

Kate's comment: I was carrying out some research for a client recently, and was having difficulty tracking down the birth of one of the client's sisters. The family were all very proud of their London roots but I could not find the sister's registration there. The only likely person that I could find was registered in Buckinghamshire. The date was 1942. On a hunch I rang the client and asked if the family had been evacuated during the war. They had – to Buckinghamshire - and my asking led to the client remembering that his sister had been born in that county!.

Copies of original marriage certificates signed by the couple and their witnesses are held in the original church register and as a copy sent to the Superintendent Registrar, but a transcript (written copy) only was sent to the GRO. If you get a copy of a marriage certificate from the GRO, it will either be a photocopy of the transcript they hold in their records or a handwritten copy of the transcript made by GRO staff. So if you want to see a copy showing your ancestor's actual signatures – or their mark – you will have to apply to the relevant Superintendent Registrar or if you are able to, look at the original marriage records for the parish.

Trap 32. You didn't make best use of the registration indexes

The great Homer Simpson once said: "If something is hard, then it is probably not worth doing." Whilst most of us probably wouldn't wholeheartedly agree with that sentiment, when it comes to trying to locate your ancestors in the indexes, he may have a point. Fortunately, the days have now gone when you had to do a manual search of the registration indexes quarter by quarter. Computerisation of the central indexes means they are now fully searchable at the click of a button. It does help, however, when using birth, marriage and death records, that you have an understanding of what is available and how you can get hold of it.

There are two sets of original indexes held in the UK; one in the district register offices and a set is held by the General Register Office. Each has a separate system for indexing and the reference for a GRO copy will not help you obtain a certificate from the district register office. It is not possible nowadays to search these records in person, but most people search on-line indexes through free or subscription-based sites. For the less computer literate there are microfiche or CD-ROM copies at places such as the National Archives at Kew; various major libraries, LDS Family History Centres which are run by the Church of the Latter Day Saints.

Some local register offices will have their indexes on line. These are often not complete, however, and so a search which returns a nil result doesn't necessarily mean that the event you are searching for did not happen there; it may be that the date it took place is not yet included in the on-line data.

Once you have identified an entry in the indexes and you are satisfied that this is the certificate you want, this can be ordered on-line through the GRO or by post, provided you use the GRO's own order form. As an alternative you can visit the actual register office where the event took place and make use of their certificate ordering service. Some local offices also offer a telephone and/or postal service. But remember that the reference numbers are different for the General Registration Indexes and those indexed locally, so you need to ensure that you do not request a certificate using a GRO Index reference from a local register office and vice versa.

> **Toni's tip:** *If you are making use of an on-line index to locate an entry always make sure that you check the transcribed reference against the actual reference shown on the image of the relevant page in the index before ordering certificates. If the reference is wrong you may not get the right certificate or any certificate at all!.*

A major problem which needs to be borne in mind when using index transcripts is the possibility of transcription error. Each stage in the process, from the original recording of names through to the production of an on-line index allows for potential mistakes to be made, despite the best efforts of the individuals involved. Considering all the possibilities for error, especially when trying to read difficult handwriting, it is a wonder that so many entries are accurate. To illustrate, if just one person in the chain misreads or mistypes an entry, then a name like 'Pope' could be changed to 'Pipe', thus making it considerably more difficult to find.

Although the certificates are invaluable for finding out things like the name of your ancestor's parents, it is possible to extract information from the indexes alone. For example, if you find a husband and wife on the census and want to find out the maiden surname of the wife, it is usually possible to do so without buying the certificate, notwithstanding the fact that the indexes did not record spouse surnames until March quarter 1912.

You can find this information because the GRO indexes have been transcribed into searchable on-line indexes by organisations such as FreeBMD. So although the spouse names were recorded separately under each surname, they were each allocated the reference number taken from the page of the marriage register. Before 1852, up to four marriages were entered on each page of the register but after that generally there are two marriages per page. Therefore, searching under the reference number will give you the names of 4 or 8 people who appear on the original register page. It is not possible to say from the index alone which person married whom, but if you have other information to go on, such as a first name, then if you are lucky there will be only one person with that first name in the list and therefore that is likely to be the person you are looking for.

"I don't care if it takes 3 fathers and 17 mothers to make a baby on your planet, my form requires ONE mother and ONE father!"

Occasionally you will find that the person you are looking for is not there or there may be five or nine names where there should be four or eight; this is generally down to transcription error and in this event to confirm the spouse name, you will need to order the certificate.

Trap 33. I got the wrong certificate

Ordering certificates can be a costly business, so you will want to take care to ensure that you get the right one. Of course this is easier said than done, and sometimes, however careful you are, you will end up getting the wrong one. This may be because you thought you had correctly identified your relative, or because you hoped it was the right person but it turned out not to be. The danger in getting the wrong certificate is, of course, that you might believe you have the right one, and end up researching the wrong family line completely.

Kate's comment: Websites exist which offer an exchange facility for people to recycle any unwanted birth, marriage and death certificates. Any certificate obtained by you in error will be of no use to you but may well be valuable to someone else. It can be worth looking on those exchange sites yourself, before sending off for any certificates. It is a long shot, but you might be able to find that one you want or could be useful to you is on the exchange list

Toni says:

"Right at the very beginning of my family history research I ordered what I thought was my great-great grandfather's birth certificate. His name was Reuben Acott and from the little information I already had I knew he was born around the middle of the 19th century. By doing a manual search of the birth indexes I thought I had found what I was looking for. With such an unusual name there was only one contender – a Reuben Acott born in 1845. I duly ordered the certificate and it came back showing he was illegitimate and born in Gloucestershire. This was a surprise to my father, who had always been told that the family had come from Kent. A short while later a distant cousin got in touch, who sent me some family information. This showed that Reuben was born in 1841 in Kent! My cousin had got this information from her mother, who was very clear on this fact. So I looked at the indexes again. I couldn't find another Reuben Acott, but what I did find was a child who was registered as 'Male Acott' born in 1841 in Kent. This of course was my man."

This illustrates two things. Firstly, just because you can only find one person with the right name, this does not mean that he/she is definitely your relative. Secondly, you should always look out for entries that just say 'male' or 'female'. In the early days of civil registration it was quite common for a child to be registered before they had been given their name. In fact, in the first quarter that civil registration was introduced, some 3762 were registered just under their surnames with the forename showing as 'female' and 4028 were just registered as 'male.' It was possible for up to 12 months after registration for a name to be added and birth certificates have an additional column for just this occurrence. One reason for not giving a child a name on registration is if they had already died, as was often the case, but it is not a good idea to automatically assume that if there was no first name the child had died; a large number of children were not formally named until their baptism.

Sometimes the certificate index reference is not readable with clarity so it is not worth the risk of sending for a certificate on a 'best guess' basis. Instead you will need to contact the General Register Office (GRO) either by telephone or post and ask them for help.

On occasions the GRO can make mistakes and send you a certificate which bears no relation to what you were expecting. One likely reason for this is GRO references are not unique, for example, the same reference will be shared by all marriages on the same page submitted by the local Registrar for indexing. So if an error has been made, it is probably where the GRO have omitted to check the name given on your certificate order and have issued a certificate with the right reference but for the wrong people.

Toni's tip: *Don't assume that if the wrong certificate has been sent to you, that the fault lies with you. The GRO offer an excellent service but just occasionally things can go wrong, so always keep a record of what you have ordered, and if the mistake does lie with the GRO then you can contact them and request a reissue of the correct certificate.*

If you are looking for a certificate for someone with a middle name, such as William Thomas Simpson, check too for registrations for William Simpson. Often second or middle names were not included during registration but added when the child was baptised. Perhaps kindly vicars at the baptism of memorably named children like Gary Baldy or Wayne Kerr would have suggested that a middle name was a good idea.

Trap 34. Which John Smith?

For those of you who have been blessed with an ancestor whose name is John Smith, then you have your work cut out for you when identifying which is the right certificate to order from the birth indexes. A name like Michael Green or John Smith is going to give you potentially thousands of individuals to choose from and so you will need to narrow down your options as much as possible before making your selection.

"He was proud to be called John Smith. Just like his father, his father's father, and his father's, father's father, oblivious to the angst he would cause to future family historians."

The first thing to do would be to pin down as closely as possible the date when he was born, using other sources where available, such as age given on the census or in other family documents, for example, date of birth listed in a family bible. Other options, although they are not always reliable, are gravestones which often give a date of birth, or at least the date of death and the age of the deceased. After 1866 death certificates give an age at death, and after 1969 they provide a date of birth as well. A death certificate may help to narrow down the location of a burial and possible gravestone, which can give additional information.

The next thing to establish would be the area in which he was born. Again, the census can be a great help here as the individual entries show a place of birth, which should lead you to a registration district. It is a good idea to check registration district boundaries to ensure you are in the correct area. If you know of any siblings, particularly if they have been given a more unusual name, then it is a good idea to look for their entries as well, as the registration district will often be the same.

After September 1911 the maiden name of the mother was included in the birth registration index which makes it easier to narrow down the search if you know who she was. Even if your person was born before this date, he may have a sibling born after 1911 which may be easier to find and will also give you a pointer towards the correct registration district.

Kate's comment: If you are unable to identify the right certificate for your ancestor, consider obtaining a copy of a sibling's certificate, preferably one with a less common first name – it will still provide parent information (although you will need to check for evidence that it is the same mother for both).

Even after you have carried out the above process, you may still have a number of contenders on the index. This is where you need to 'kill off' the surplus, by checking the death registers to see if any death registrations have occurred soon after birth. With high infant mortality rates in the past it is quite possible to reduce your list of contenders in this way.

Toni's tip: It is good practice to check the death registers before you order a birth certificate as a matter of course. You might think you have correctly identified the birth registration, even if you are researching a fairly unusual name, but by checking you may avoid buying an unnecessary certificate. You may have found a cousin or even someone who is not directly related at all.

Sherlock Holmes is often quoted as saying: "When you have elimi-nated the impossible, whatever remains, however improbable, must be the truth." but we have found this can be an expensive and long-winded process in terms of ancestor-hunting! Unless the GRO reinstate their useful but now defunct reference checking service, the only way around this is to bite the bullet by identifying contending certificates in a priority order, then get each certificate one-by-one, reviewing each before going onto the next.

Trap 35. He never seems to have been born

Calling a child by an unusual name like Horatio Bonaventure Stevens should make it easier for a family historian to follow him, but not so if you can't find his birth in the indexes. There are several reasons for why he may not be there. For example, before 1875 it was estimated that for one reason or another around 7% of births weren't recorded, but it is more likely is that mistakes have been made in transcription or recording. This of course could be complicated by different spellings used during his lifetime. So if you take dear old Horatio, his surname of Stevens could have several variants; the name Horatio when seen written poorly could look like Horace; the middle name might not have been recorded at all and before you know it, he has become Horace Stephen and suddenly hard to find.

We have said before how children were often recorded as just 'male' or 'female' with their surname, and this can make them hard to find. We have come across several instances where a child was given one name at registration but subsequently given another at baptism or even later. One such individual was Dennis Edwin Turner, born around 1861. His entire existence was very hard to establish because of the different names he went under throughout his lifetime.

Family legend had it that he had gone under the name of Tanner but searches of the General Register Indexes for his birth failed to bring up either a Dennis Edwin Turner or Tanner. By a stroke of luck we stumbled across a baptism entry in the parish records for an eight month old Dennis Edwin Tanner. This baptism took place at Maidstone on 13th October 1861 and showed a John and Eliza Tanner as grandparents. No parent was named. However, the 1861 census showed that John and Eliza had a grandson of the correct age living with them – but his name was Thomas. A check on the General Register Indexes showed no child by the name of Thomas Tanner being registered in the right area at the right time, either for a birth or a death. But there was an entry for a 'male Tanner' for the March 1861 quarter and the indications were that this is the child we sought.

Dennis Edwin Turner certainly existed – he appears on the 1891 and 1901 census but not on any others. No Thomas Tanner who could potentially be our candidate appeared after 1861 on any census. So what has happened here? The most likely explanation is that the child that Eliza and John had baptised was an illegitimate offspring of one of their children. But it seems that the family simply could not decide what they wanted to call him. He was registered as 'Male Tanner', called Thomas for a while - at least during the time of the 1861 census - and finally Dennis Edwin was settled on when it came to his baptism.

Toni's tip: *Once you have exhausted all spelling variants and phonetic searches in the registration indexes, you could try again but with minimal information. Less is sometimes more with search engines. You could try the following search ideas:*

- *If the birth is after September 1911, try searching with the mother's maiden surname plus the surname of the child. Even if the child you are seeking doesn't pop up, a sibling might, and their certificate may give you clues for taking the family further back. If this doesn't work try the mother's maiden name and the first name of the child. Again, this can be narrowed by area and/or time period as appropriate.*
- *Child's surname only for the time period you are interested in;*
- *Child's surname only for the area you think they were born in such as county or district (without a time period);*
- *Child's surname only (only really feasible for uncommon surnames)*
- *Depending on how common it is, also try the child's first name only, but you will usually need to narrow it to the area and time period you are interested in.*

You may not find a birth entry in the GRO indexes for someone because they have later given incorrect information on a census which you take as fact. For example, we know of a John Edward Myers who appears on several censuses, stating his place of birth to be Wapping, but in fact he turns out to be a German national who has come to Britain, anglicised his name and whether as a misunder-standing or a deliberate effort to mislead the authorities, claimed to have been born in London.

Notwithstanding the difficult cases illustrated above, the census still remains the most effective and useful tool for locating the birth place of someone and by corroborating this information with records held by the GRO you can be fairly assured that you have the correct person. Most problems with locating people really are due to mis-spellings and transcription errors so it pays to be as imaginative as possible with spelling variants and don't limit your searches to phonetic searches only.

"The Right Honourable Percival Harrington de Mansfield Twizlington-Smythe? Sorry sir, I'll have to shorten that to fit in the box. I'll say Percy Smith, OK?"

If your family has a double-barrelled name, such as the afore-mentioned Harrison-Chinn family, then the GRO indexes these alphabetically after the Harrison entries. Harrison-Chinn will appear after Harrison-Bates but before Harrison-Graves. Occasionally a Registrar will assume the first part of the surname, in this case, Harrison, is a middle name and so if you were looking for a Paul Harrison-Chinn he may be indexed not under 'H' for Harrison but as Paul Harrison Chinn under 'C' for Chinn. Sometimes if a Registrar is unsure he would enter them under both variations so they would appear twice.

Names of Irish origins such as O'Reilly appear alphabetically as if the apostrophe does not exist so O'Reilly would appear between Orange and Organ. The Scottish Mc and Mac are not so straight-forward. Before the June quarter of 1969 they were indexed separately. After this date they are all indexed as MAC, so both McDonald and MacDonald are indexed under Mac.

If you are having serious problems in locating an entry for someone you are sure should appear on the registers, then it might be worth in-vestigating whether or not he was born in the UK. Separate indexes are held by the GRO for entries involving Britons who were born abroad.

Trap 36. They can't have married

Oscar Wilde is quoted as saying that "Bigamy is having one wife too many. Monogamy is the same." Whilst we can say that dear old Oscar wasn't strictly the marrying kind, there are those that found the whole process somewhat of an addiction. Take the example of Mr Gloucester Gale who had a very busy 9 months in the late 1850's. He made an appearance at the Old Bailey for feloniously marrying Martha Gover on 3rd July, 1858, when he was already married. His crimes didn't stop there, as in the same court case he was also indicted of feloniously marrying Fanny Turrell on 17th August, 1858; Sarah Ann Drewett on 3rd May, 1858; Lydia March on 3rd January, 1858; and Cecilia Maria Wye, on 30th November, 1857. To his credit he pleaded guilty to all charges and received four years penal servitude as his reward.

It is always thought that the Victorians were highly moral and respectability was very important to them. It is therefore somewhat surprising to find out that many couples from this time were not married. A huge proportion of those who did marry did so when it was found that the lady in question was pregnant, although sometimes

"I'm sorry, Mr Gale, but we don't offer a discount for bulk purchase of wedding rings."

the marriage did not take place until after the baby was born – in some cases when their children were quite old.

As divorce was not an option for most people, the person you married was the person you were bound to for the rest of your natural lives. So you can understand the reason for caution when considering marriage.

So why didn't people marry in order to be wholly respectable if they were already living together as man and wife? One common reason for not marrying was that one or both parties were already married. A divorce was difficult to achieve, as prior to 1857 you had to pay for a private Act of Parliament to be passed in order to divorce. This was a slow, costly affair and not really an option for many people. So the easier option was to leave your existing spouse and just live with the new partner in your life.

We have come across examples where a couple, living together as man and wife, have eventually married when the death of an earlier spouse has occurred. What is not known is whether the children of the later relationship were aware of their parents' secret. It was safer to live together and run the risk of this being discovered, rather than being charged with bigamy. Prison sentences were usually given for proven cases of bigamy. Usually it was men who were punished but women were sometimes found out, too. A rather unfortunate case was Elizabeth Wood Lloyd who in 1826 was sentenced to seven years transportation to Australia – by no means a lenient sentence. Her misfortune was to marry before her first husband had died, even though he was not seemingly a very nice person. It was discovered in court that at one stage he had 'sold' his wife to a sailor named Bligh for a bottle of wine and 5 shillings!

Toni's tip: If you are using a searchable marriage index and are looking for an entry using both full names but have been unsuccessful, try just one full name and just the forename of the other. It may be that one surname is recorded incorrectly. If this doesn't work, try the other partner's full name and the forename of the other. Other things to try include searching on one name only (preferably the more unusual of the pair); extending the search beyond the time period which you think is probable; using the phonetic sound option; or if the forenames of the pair are fairly distinct try a forename search for both only – but you will probably have to narrow the search to the area you think they may have married, and restrict the time period.

Another reason for a couple not marrying to avoid breaking the law is that of consanguinity, or in other words, how closely related the couple are. Obviously you cannot, and usually wouldn't want to, marry your sister/mother/father and so on, but perhaps it is not so obvious that before 1907 it was illegal to marry your dead wife's sister and before 1921 you couldn't marry your dead brother's wife. No doubt many people found comfort in the arms of a dead spouse's sibling but they were unable to legalise such a union.

Generally if a couple got married then it is perfectly straightforward to find a record of their marriage in the GRO indexes. If the one you are looking for cannot be found, then this may well be because they never married or because the marriage took place much later than you expected. So whilst you might think your ancestors were above reproach, you might find that there was more than one marriage, a late marriage or no marriage at all.

However, before you decide they were an immoral lot who cared little for convention, you might like to consider that perhaps your search processes need a little tweaking. For instance, the woman could marry more than once after being widowed and you might be searching for her marriage under her maiden name whereas she may have married under one of her married names.

And in case you are wondering just how Gloucester Gale got away with all his extra marriages, well, he used assumed names for each marriage so the authorities did not pick them up. But more to the point, how did he get away with his frequent absences from each wife? He pretended to them that he was a Mate aboard a merchant ship trading around Europe. One wonders whether he suffered from exhaustion, and this we don't know, but it was reported at the time of the trial that he couldn't walk without the aid of a stick.

Trap 37. They vanish off the face of the earth

No matter what medical procedures, healthy living and magical potions we try out, eventually for us The Time Is Up, unless of course you are Dr Who, a Deity, Vampire or some other 'Immortal Being'. So given that every person who has lived has to die, it seems extraordinary that we cannot find death records for some of our forebears.

Certain things we can discount as improbable, such as alien abduction, and there are probably occasions where an ancestor may die suddenly away from home and his name not known to the authorities so no accurate death registration can be made. Parish Registers do sometimes show entries such as 'a stranger found dead' or 'unknown man found on beach,' but there are usually less exceptional, straightforward reasons for people's deaths not being found. People do sometimes disappear, perhaps by foul means, or they simply decide to start a new life elsewhere, perhaps under a different name.

But generally, we are able to find our ancestor's birth, subsequent marriage, birth of children and using census data other things such as where they lived, what they did: so why then does the situation arise whereby the person concerned fails to appear on a census, the surviving spouse is described as widow/widower and yet we can't find an entry for that person in the death indexes? Or sometimes we have just one snippet of information, the birth registration, then absolutely nothing after this. How can this happen?

Really, they should be there. Errors in recording or transcription can be the reasons you cannot find them. One of the methods we suggest you try is that of using a search of the transcription indexes based on phonetics - in other words, the way the name sounds when pronounced, rather than the way it is spelt. Unfortunately this is not as straightforward as it seems, as many data bases use a system known as Soundex, which research has shown is far from perfect. Tests have shown that around one-third of matches using this system were incorrect and a quarter of matches were not identified.

Soundex is based on a system of substituting letters for ones that sound similar. It is not based on a list drawn up by someone linking names by how they sound. It uses a system which keeps the first letter of the name the same, but subsequent letters are awarded a number according to a set of rules based on the sound, and letters with the same number code are substituted. So the letters B, F, P and V are awarded the numerical code 1; C, G, J, K, Q, S, X and Z are given the code number 2 and so on. So if you did a Soundex search on a name like Tapp, you will get results such as Tabb or Taff but not necessarily Tape or Tipp. Because of the limitations of keeping the first letter of the name, a phonetic search of the name Haycock will not give Acock or any of the known variations of this name. To be fair, many family history websites recognise the problems with Soundex but at present there is no better alternative.

Toni's tip: You may find it helpful to compile a list of all known variations of the names you are searching and keep it handy so that you can be thorough and methodical in your searching.

Kate's comment: I have had many examples of failures of a phonetic search to locate someone but when trying my own variations of the name, have found it. I was looking for someone recently with the name Piper – they just couldn't be found and the phonetic search was giving me Pipper, Pyper and a few weird variations. Eventually I found them listed as Paper. I found this not by using a phonetic search but by thinking what a mis-transcribed letter 'i' could look like. I decided it could either look like an 'a' or an 'e' or an 'o' and so was prepared to search for Paper, Peper or Poper, and found it as Paper.

If you are trying to locate someone that you know something about but who seems to vanish later on, try and pin down marriage records or birth of children; this may lead you to a change of name or location which may help.

It is worth considering that your missing person may have emigrated or gone abroad for a while. There are many passenger lists for people travelling abroad available on-line. If your person cannot be found on any outgoing lists it is worth checking inbound lists as you might not catch them going out but may get them coming back for a visit! If they joined the army they may have been posted abroad, married or died there.

If you believe that the person was in the Services and died in either world war, you can check the Commonwealth War Graves Commission Index which will help determine whether this is the case, and if so, where they died and where their grave will be.

> *Toni's tip:* If all else fails and you still have an ancestor who vanishes from the GRO indexes, then try checking with the register office in the locality where you expect to find them. Just occasionally an entry will be missed off the GRO index, although this is probably a bit of a long shot.

If all else fails, under the Freedom of Information Act it is now possible to look in the military files which detail investigations into sightings of Unidentified Flying Objects, and it may be able to correlate sightings with the last known location of your missing ancestor . . . well, you never know!

Trap 38. Right certificate, details not as expected

There is always a little thrill of anticipation when the envelope from the GRO containing a birth, marriage or death certificate plops through the letterbox. You never know what details will be revealed and where these details will lead you. So imagine if you are sending off for your great-grandfather's wedding certificate. You open it to find his wife is called Sarah. This is completely unexpected because you know from other documentation that she was called Anne. What you hoped to get from this certificate was her maiden surname and suddenly you are faced with a conundrum – who was Sarah? Why does your other, valid evidence tell you her name was Anne?

So you do all the other checks – did Sarah die soon and Great-Grandad remarry in a very short space of time? Was Anne a nickname or second name? Have you got the wrong marriage certificate? If the answer to these questions is 'no' then you must then ask yourself why the information on the certificate is not as expected.

There is always the possibility that the Registrar has got it wrong. He may have misheard or misunderstood information given to him or had for some mysterious reason been given incorrect information. One case we have come across is of a man giving his occupation as hairdresser on two census records. When a birth certificate for one of his children arrived, however, he was shown as being a french polisher. Luckily, a baptism record was available for the same child that gave the occupation of father as hairdresser, and the address at baptism was the same address recorded on the birth certificate. The initial doubts that we may have got the wrong child were alleviated but it still remained a mystery. So we need to question whether it is likely that the father would have had two completely unrelated occupations, assuming he didn't french polish bald heads as an extra hairdressing service.

Toni's tip: Do try to get to the bottom of any inconsistencies you find, otherwise you may find out some way down the line that the certificate is not for who you think it is and you have been researching someone else's family tree.

On occasions the person shown as the father on a marriage certificate is incorrect. This may happen when the person getting married has been brought up by a person other than their natural father but believes him to be their actual father, not knowing that he is a stepfather. Sometimes an illegitimate person will have given a stepfather's, brother's or grandfather's name as an actual father. Alternatively they may simply make up a name, perhaps saying they are deceased to dodge awkward questions. They would do this to avoid the embarrassment or stigma of leaving the 'father' column blank. Any of these scenarios can be extremely frustrating for a family historian to sort out.

The ages stated on a marriage certificate can also be very misleading. Often a certificate will just say 'full age' which means the person marrying is 21 or over, which is very unhelpful, as they could be 81 for all we know! In other situations the bride or groom might deliberately tell an untruth about their age, either because they were too young to marry without parental consent, in other words, under the age of 21. If there was a wide gap in ages between the happy couple they might knock off a few years of his age to make the gap less wide. Sometimes the bride was older than the groom and she would therefore shave a few years off to make the gap seem less of a chasm. In one case known to us the bride managed to not so much shave, but bulldoze, 18 years off in this way!

Kate's comment: If you have been researching your family for some time you will probably already know that situations could change quite quickly for a family. For example, occupations could change or different first names used. Frequent changes of address can also occur, sometimes rapidly – as often as monthly in some cases, perhaps where people were trying to keep one step ahead of the landlord!

Sometimes very strange anomalies occur and in those cases the only thing you can do is make a 'best guess' as to what has happened. To illustrate, Toni was carrying out some research on behalf of the Cremer family:

"I was given a photocopy of a birth certificate by a client. The father was correctly recorded as William Henry Cremer, but there was a gap where the mother's maiden name should have been, so that it read 'Alice Cremer, formerly 'blank'. Looking closely I could see that something like a piece of paper had been put over the former surname to block it out on the photocopy which was very odd. When I looked in the birth indexes I could see that the maiden name of the mother was 'Hill' – this was astonishing as 'Hill' was the name of William Henry's first wife, who was long gone by this time. I knew from army records that this wife had been abandoned by William Henry some time before and they no longer had any contact. So how could this estranged Alice appear on the indexes as the mother? We will probably never know but the most likely explanation is that it was a complete misunderstanding by the father who actually had registered the birth. Both of William Henry's two wives were called Alice so perhaps he just got a bit confused and gave the wrong maiden name for the current Alice. If this is the case he was probably not very popular with the second wife when she saw what was on the certificate!"

Trap 39. Not using every scrap of information

Assuming that you are applying for a birth or marriage certificate to help you with your family research rather than to assist you with a sophisticated identity theft, you will be doing so to find out details such as parents' names in order to get back another generation. If this is the only information you take from the certificate, however, you might be overlooking a really useful resource which can tell you a lot about your family background.

The occupation of the father on certificates can often help you pinpoint the individual on the census with accuracy. Even death certificates sometimes yield useful information, for example, we once had a death certificate which showed the place of death as being 204 Hoxton Street, Shoreditch. Some investigation of this address told us that this was the workhouse at the time, which opened up a new avenue of research.

Extra information can be extracted from marriage certificates. Marriages generally took place in the church belonging to the Parish where the woman came from, which can be a helpful pointer to where she was living prior to marriage. It is worth checking baptism records for that church as well, as not only may she have been baptised there but also any children of the marriage may well have been baptised there too. The certificate for the marriage may also have helpful details as to whether the church was non-conformist, e.g. Baptist, which helps when looking through Parish records for evidence of the family. If you look at the line which reads '... according to the rites and ceremonies ...' this may indicate a non-conformist religion. If the marriage took place at what looks like a home address this could indicate that the couple had a Quaker or Jewish wedding. Care should be exercised with Scottish weddings, however, as these often took place in the home so the same inference cannot be drawn.

If the certificate shows one or both of the couple to be 'minors' this meant that they required a parent's permission in order to marry. The age for consent has changed over the years; when registration first began in 1837, a girl could marry at 12 years and a boy at 14, although very few did. This was only changed as late as 1926 when the age of consent was raised to 16. Parental permission was still required to marry until the person was 21 but this was reduced to 18 later.

Generally if a father of the marrying couple had died before they were married, then the certificate should show the word 'dec' or 'deceased' after his name, but again this cannot be relied upon because it was often overlooked.

You may come across a marriage certificate which shows that the couple married by Licence, not by Banns. Banns delayed a wedding by several weeks but were cheap, whereas Licences were quick but more costly. This practice occurred for a few different reasons. Sometimes the bride was pregnant and the couple wished for the marriage to take place as quickly as possible in order to disguise the fact that they 'had' to get married. Licences were also used where the couple wanted to get married in a place of their choice but which wasn't the parish in which either of them lived. Because of the cost of the Licence there was a certain amount of status value attached to it – if the couple could afford it, then they would marry that way in order to show they had available money for such a luxury. If the actual Licence can be tracked down they can often give extra information for the family historian.

It is always worth looking to see who the witnesses are on a marriage certificate. Sometimes these names can be used to confirm you have the right family as they may be brothers or sisters, or other family members. Sometimes they can be work colleagues or neighbours which when cross-referenced to the census can give you that little extra evidence that you have the right people.

> *Toni's tip:* Look through your birth, marriage and death certificates from time-to-time, as sometimes an address or some other piece of information that didn't seem important when you initially received the certificate can suddenly come into its own – perhaps confirming or disproving information you have more recently found.

Death certificates, although generally not very informative, still can yield some valuable information. The person who informed the Registrar of the death is often a family member which again can help you pinpoint that you have the correct certificate.

If the death had been notified to the Coroner it may be possible to track down his records for further information. Similarly if the letters PM appear on the certificate you know that a Post Mortem examination will have taken place and again records of this may still exist.

By 1845 if the cause of death has the word 'Certified' after it this tells you that a doctor had established the cause of death. If this word does not appear this lets you know that the diagnosis was made by relatives or carers and that in this case they are likely to be poor. If a member of a poor family dies, then to call a doctor out to certify why they died was an expense the family could well do without. Some early diagnoses of cause of death probably wouldn't satisfy a coroner nowadays. As some 17th century records have shown, it was deemed quite possible to die of hysteria, surfeit, recklessness or lethargy!

Trap 40. You ignore deaths

While death is the only certain thing which will occur to someone once they have been born, deaths are often overlooked by genealogists as not being of much use. In fact, many family trees fail to have dates of death on them. It is almost as if once someone was born, married and had children they were no longer of interest.

This is a shame as many interesting things can be gained from a death certificate. You will get information on date of death, cause and place, post-1866 the age at death, and post-1969 the date of birth. Death certificates have the potential to reveal more than these facts, however.

A home address gives you the opportunity to locate the family on a census. It may also help you locate another family member if they were living at the same address. Sometimes getting the death certificate can be used to obtain the correct birth certificate for an individual, if there had been a few candidates to choose from and no other evidence to help you decide.

If you are very lucky (although probably not lucky for the deceased) then the death will have been referred to the Coroner and if his report still exists this can give you an immense wealth of detail on that person and their family.

Toni's tip: *If you have a 'Coroner' death, you may or may not be lucky enough to find the actual Coroner's records, however, if the death is sufficiently interesting it will most probably be reported in a local newspaper. Many of these can be searched on-line or failing this, you may be able to track these down in County and local libraries or in the British Library Newspaper archive.*

If you obtained the death certificate for Archibald Brown, of Rayleigh in Essex, you would discover that he died as a result of an explosion. As that death occurred in 1943 you would be forgiven for thinking this was as a result of enemy action but a search of the Coroner's records and newspaper accounts would reveal otherwise.

Archibald was aged 47 when his death occurred. Accounts from the time tell us that he was a short-tempered, controlling man who was confined to a wheelchair as a result of a motorcycle accident some 23 years earlier, which left him in constant pain. As 23rd July that year was a balmy summer's day, his nurse, Doris Mitchell, took him for a stroll in his chair along the Hockley Road. After about a mile she stopped and helped him to light a cigarette. As she resumed pushing, the chair exploded. Bits of Archibald were propelled into the road, with one leg ending up a nearby tree and the other being found some 16 yards away in someone's front garden. Nurse Mitchell was badly, but fortunately not fatally, injured.

The subsequent police investigation revealed that underneath the seat of the wheelchair a Hawkins No. 75 grenade mine had been placed, and that when Archibald shifted his weight after lighting his cigarette, the grenade was triggered. Not surprisingly, suspicion fell onto Archibald's son Eric, who was home from the army on compassionate leave. Eric was good with mechanical things and not only was he familiar with the Hawkins No. 75 grenade mine as a result of his army training, but he had access to them as well.

Eric was not on good terms with his father, as he and his mother were frequently bullied by the bad tempered Archibald, and it was reported that he was unstable and had lost jobs in the past as a result of this instability. Under questioning, Eric confessed to the crime and was taken to trial at the Chelmsford Assizes on 4th November 1943. He was found guilty but insane and was sent to an asylum where he remained for 32 years until his release in 1975. And if you hadn't obtained the death certificate in the first place, you might never have known about this.

One note of caution is that information about ages at death is often incorrect. This is usually because the information is naturally not given by the deceased themselves but by a friend or relative of the deceased, or the master of the workhouse where he/she has been residing. The more remote the relationship, the more vague or inaccurate the information given will be. Sometimes the deceased person will have been untruthful about their age during their lifetime or simply not known accurately where they were born or what their age was. In the early days of registration it was not important for people to know how old they were, after all, there was no compulsory schooling or old age pension so knowing your exact date of birth was not that big an issue. Rules and regulations regarding death certificates have changed throughout the years. Prior to 1875 you did not actually have to have a body in order to register the death of someone. You would go along to the Registrar, wipe a tear from your eye and sadly announce the death of your Aunty Maud. "Terribly sorry," would say the Registrar, "and here's your death certificate." The possibilities for fraud were quite significant, as there were burial clubs which you could join, and then claim money for the death of a relative (either real or invented). So an Act was passed in 1874 which meant that medical certification would be necessary to confirm someone's death. This reduced the likelihood of fraud but may not have had a positive effect on murder rates.

"Oh dear, Mrs James you must be the unluckiest bride ever, that's the third husband who's died unexpectedly this year."

CENSUS OF HUMOUR

Census problems – finding people & understanding results

Enumeration work wasn't the easy money
he'd been led to believe.

Trap 41. The census wasn't just for family history

There was opposition from religious organisations in the 18th Century when it was proposed to hold a census in Britain. The concern was that according to the Old Testament, when King David attempted a census of the Israelites, God was so annoyed he sent a plague which killed 70,000. People in Britain in the mid 1700's were worried that similar revenge would occur, should a census be undertaken. So it was quite ironic, really, that the early censuses were administered by the Overseers of the Poor, who were often churchwardens or appointed by the local gentry and the Rector.

Given that the census returns are such a valuable resource for the family historian, it can sometimes be overlooked that this was not the original purpose behind the idea of having a census. The census was developed to analyse population numbers and provide a better understanding of socio-economic factors in Britain. For over two hundred years, a census has been taken every ten years and the resulting data has been used to influence social policy and planning. England had a much earlier census - the Domesday book, commissioned by William the Conqueror in the 11th century. This was a record of people and property which had parallels with census data gathered some 900 years later.

Of course, the census records are of immense value to the family historian. Because of the 10 year gap between censuses, it is possible to build up a picture of the lives of your ancestors, following their journeys and providing details of each generation, through the decades.

Toni's tip: Keep a list handy of dates the censuses were taken. This will help you determine the correct age for people on the day of the census, and clarify where there is doubt whether someone had born or died by the time of the census. The dates are:

1841 - taken on 7 June	1871 - taken on 2 April	1901 - taken on 31 March
1851 - taken on 30 March	1881 - taken on 3 April	1911 - taken on 2 April
1861 - taken on 7 April	1891 - taken on 5 April	1921 – taken on 19 June

The first modern census was carried out in each parish in 1801 and every 10 years thereafter. Those early censuses were used for statistical data and, in the main, those from 1801, 1811, 1821 and 1831 were destroyed. There is a useful guide to those which survived, "Local Census Listings 1522-1930" by Jeremy Gibson and Mervyn Medlycott.

Kate's comment: To protect people's privacy, census data is only released to the general public after 100 years have passed. The 1911 census was released a few years early but with certain personal information not shown until the full 100 years had passed. After the 1921 census there will be a gap, as the 1931 was accidentally destroyed by fire and the 1941 census did not take place because of the disruption of World War II.

Rich pickings are available to the family history researcher from data contained in the censuses, starting with the one taken in 1841. The 1841 census is the most limited as it does not state what the relationship between household members was, nor does it give much detail on where people were born. It only states whether people were born within the county or from Scotland, Ireland or 'Foreign Parts.' It will indicate gender, occupation and where the person was living at the time of the census. However, ages for people over 15 were rounded down to the nearest 5 years, so a 24 year old could appear as aged 20. Naturally not everyone abided by the rules so sometimes ages were rounded up, some put their actual ages, some didn't know and others just didn't tell the truth. Whilst ages given on census returns are best treated with a degree of caution, those on the 1841 should generally be treated with suspicion!

As time went on, more information was requested of people, so that from 1851 census onwards you are able to determine the relationship between household members and where people were born. In 1851 a question was also included which asked whether a person was either blind or deaf-and-dumb; in 1871 this question was extended to cover whether an individual was an imbecile, idiot or lunatic. From 1891 questions were asked about the number of rooms in the house and whether a person was an employer or employed. People living in Wales were asked whether they spoke Welsh.

The 1911 census is of particular interest to the historian because of the extra information which was required. This included the length of the present marriage, how many children were born alive to that marriage, how many of those were still living and greater detail regarding occupations. It is also interesting as the individual household schedules have survived so researchers can see their ancestor's handwriting.

All censuses have been indexed and are searchable on-line through subscription-based genealogical websites but there are some free transcripts available on-line such as those on the LDS Family Search website where you can find, for example, a transcription of the entire 1881 census. However if computers aren't your thing, then old microfilm and/or microfiche copies are available for 1841 to 1901 at places such as The National Archives, many County Record Offices and LDS Family History Centres. However, the 1911 was not microfilmed but a digitalised version is available for free searching at the National Archives.

"Zark, quick it's the census enumerator! Turn the light off and pretend we are out."

Trap 42. The census enumerator got it wrong

There is a common misunderstanding about how the census was taken in its early days. It is imagined that a self-important, frock-coated enumerator hammered on the door of each hovel within his jurisdiction and demanded the names of those staying in the household that night. The reality was quite different.

Starting with the 1841 census, the pattern for census data collection was established. For a start, the enumerator would have found it quite difficult to go to each house in his district in what would be a fairly tight time scale. The country was divided into small districts that would have contained between 25 and 200 inhabited houses, the smaller number being in the more rural areas where distances between properties would have to be negotiated. Public institutions such as gaols or workhouses were enumerated separately by the officers in charge of those institutions.

A few days before the census was to be taken, a blank form, called a schedule, was delivered to every householder throughout England, Wales and Scotland. It was the responsibility of the head of each household to ensure that the schedule was completed with details of everyone who would be sleeping in his house at midnight on the specific date of the census. This would include people who were travelling and staying the night or simply visiting the family. It was the enumerator's job to collect the schedules and collate the information for their district.

Illiteracy amongst adults was common in the early days of census taking, but their children may have been attending school or Sunday school and would have learned to read and write, so the job of completing the census schedule may have passed to them. Friends or neighbours who could write were in demand to complete the schedules on behalf of others. No doubt the enumerator would find that he would have to help fill out forms for some, but the blame for mistakes cannot be attributed solely to the enumerator. Mistakes could creep in at all points of the process.

Sometimes a literate wife may have been given the job of completing the schedule. There are a few excellent examples where they have taken advantage of their less educated husband by being creative with their details, such as the woman in 1881 who gave her status as 'Maid of All Work', her occupation as 'Slave' and her handicap as 'Scarcity of Money.' In 1851 the rumour that a woman in Portsmouth had declared herself as head of household had reached the newspapers. Apparently she had given her occupation as 'Mangle worker' and listed her husband's occupation as 'turns my mangle.' Whilst this was newsworthy, she wasn't the first woman to be head of household over her husband – Queen Victoria was shown as Head in 1841, even though her husband, Prince Albert, was around at the time.

In the week following census night, the enumerator would collect the household schedules. Failure to comply ran the risk of a financial penalty. Once collected, the enumerator would transfer the details from the individual household schedules into his own consolidated schedule, known as the enumerator's book. The enumerator's book would be examined by the Registrars and submitted to the Superintendent Registrars for countersigning. From here they were sent to the General Register Office where the required statistical data would be extracted, and the original schedules were destroyed (apart from those used for the 1911).

During this process of compiling and checking of data, many ticks and marks were made on the pages, and often these would be made over personal information. As a result some data, such as ages, can be difficult to read.

Toni's tip: *If you are expecting to find your ancestors in a particular village, but they don't seem to be indexed there or anywhere else, look through all the households in the village in question. Most service providers provide the facility for you to do a page-by-page search for a particular location – you may find them this way, perhaps mis-indexed. Unfortunately this is not so practical if all you know is that the family were in London!*

Some of the data that had to be collated by the enumerators must have caused them to raise an eyebrow at the very least! For example, some of the occupations given on the returns have included gems such as 'professional wizard', a 'Punch and Judy man', and a 'retired opium smuggler'. A favourite has to be the man who gave his occupation as being 'Generally Useful' although at least we can work out roughly what this means. Bizarrely, one street in Cornwall boasted a retired smuggler just a few doors away from a retired customs officer. You can't help wondering whether they popped into the local pub for a drink and talked of old times together!

Trap 43. Believing the census index is right

Before the advent of computerised indexes for census data, family historians would have to painstakingly search microfilm or microfiche records for evidence of their ancestors. This would be fairly straight-forward if their ancestors obligingly stayed in the same village throughout the generations. There is an idea that people did not move around very much but the opposite was often the case. People may have moved short distances to neighbouring villages or migrated much further for a host of reasons, but generally to find work or because they married into a family already established elsewhere. Many London families moved house incredibly frequently and although they may have travelled only a short distance, this would easily take them into other enumeration districts. To find a family in London, therefore, could be the work of many days, hunched over the reading equipment, systematically searching district after district. It is no wonder, then, that as soon as the technology existed, historians jumped on the chance of having searchable indexes for the censuses.

Attempts at indexing have been made over the last 30 years or so, often carried out by local family history societies. However, these indexes in the main have been superseded by national on-line indexes.

The first attempt to produce a national indexed census was jointly carried out by the Church of Jesus Christ of Latter Day Saints and the Federation of Family History Societies. Their project called for volunteers to transcribe the 1881 census. Strict rules were in place to minimise transcription errors, so two volunteers independently transcribed a section, and their transcriptions were compared by a third person to ensure their transcriptions tallied and they would sort out any discrepancy. Toni says: "As one of the volunteers on this project, I had the task of transcribing the details for Palgrave, in Suffolk – so I offer my apologies should anyone think I have mis-transcribed their ancestors!"

The next project was commissioned by a forward-thinking Public Record Office, now known as the National Archives. They decided to make the 1901 census available to the public via the Internet. This was an ambitious project as it included not just the transcription and indexing but also included links to the original census pages.

However, they did not have the resources to undertake this project themselves so they outsourced it to a sub-contractor under a Private Finance Initiative. This subcontractor was the Enterprise and Supply Services, which was a division of H M Prison services. Agreements were made with individual prisoners to transcribe portions of the census.

Unfortunately, progress on the 1901 transcription was slow, so the work was eventually further sub-contracted out, reputedly to the Indian subcontinent. The cost of this work was more than the Enterprise and Supply Services had received to do the work in the first place. It will probably come as no great surprise to learn that the final transcription was riddled with errors and family historians generally found many causes for complaint. In addition, when it was published on-line, the service could not cope with the massive interest in it and the system collapsed. The service was withdrawn for eight months until the initial wrinkles were ironed out. Lessons were learned from this project so that later transcriptions were much more accurate, although errors do occur.

Kate's comment: A name index generally differs from a transcript. An index may just contain minimal information, for example, names and ages, whereas a transcript has more fields included. Some commercial companies offer the choice of a compre-hensive transcript or the actual image itself. Although it is important to always check back to the original, it is often quicker and sometimes cheaper (if paying per view) to find the person you are looking for on the transcript, and if this looks right, then check on the original image. This is because the tran-scriptions usually load much faster for you to check than waiting for each original image to load on your browser. This is especially useful to people who experience difficulties in getting fast Internet downloads.

It should not be surprising that errors are made considering the huge amount of data that has to be transcribed for each census. As population numbers increase year-on-year, each successive census gets larger, with correspondingly more data to transcribe. The headcount for England and Wales in 1841 was around 15 million, whereas the current population is four times that, at just over 60 million. If the indexing is outsourced to overseas workers, which is very likely for cost reasons, then the transcribers are unlikely to be familiar with English names and place names, allowing for 'best guesses' rather than accuracy. Commercial pressures to get the job done in a given time may compound these difficulties.

> **Toni's tip:** *If you do find your ancestor has been incorrectly indexed, submit a correction to the service provider, so others do not have the same problem.*

Commercial websites with on-line census records tend to be secretive about how their indexing is carried out. At least one major organisation, however, works by digitising the original microfilm and then outsources these images to be transcribed by partner organisations, by using specialist software and manual keying. The keyed contents of completed batches are returned to the commissioning organisation for checking, with failed batches being returned to the partners for re-keying.

Because of the human input into this process, errors will always creep in, but it should not be underestimated just how useful these indexes are. On a good day with a reasonably distinctive name, it is possible to build a family tree extending back over 200 years in just an afternoon – something that would have been considered virtually impossible only 10 years ago.

Trap 44. Your census searches are ineffective

Picture the scene. It is 2021 and the census is taking place. Ryan has gone to Glasgow with his mates to work. Ryan is a brilliant plasterer but didn't do very well at school and struggled with forms all his life. So the landlord in the B&B where he is staying is filling in his details for him. What Ryan said was 'Southend, mate. It's in Essex.' What the Landlord heard was 'Sowfendmayte'. 130 years later, Ryan's descendent is searching old maps and data files in vain to find where in Essex that the town of Sowfendmayte was. Not being able to find it, he decides that no such place exists and he gives up the search.

However, with a bit of thinking around the subject, Ryan's descendent could have sorted out the problem by using his genetically enhanced server monkey to do a DNA search whilst he went to the local spaceport by jetpack and boarded a holiday flight to Jupiter. However, in the absence of such technology, we have to use a more basic approach. It may be that by excluding the term 'Sowfendmayte' and concentrating on the other information we know about Ryan, he may just pop up. However, sometimes we need a more lateral approach and this is where understanding how present-day search engines work is useful.

If you are using an on-line subscription service, it will help you immensely if you understand how their search results are presented. There is no industry standard and each provider has its own methods. Some will default to displaying exact matches to your search terms, whereas others will give you a wider range of results. Where a wider range is given, the results are typically given in an ascending order of closeness to your request. It is usually possible to restrict a search to match your criteria exactly, but it can be useful to have alternative choices to look at, even if wading through hundreds of less relevant results can be a slog.

You can make these 'inexact' matches work for you if you are aware of the order of priority which your data is used by the search engine. Most systems will look for exact matches first, but failing this, which criteria will they sort the results by? If you search on a surname, age and place of birth, and don't have an exact match, will the search engine look for people with the correct age (or nearest), or place of birth, or alternative name spellings first? If you selected a '+ or − 2' years either side of the 'age' option, will the results given to you show a five-year age range as a priority over the place of birth results? If you know the system you are using gives priority to the age field over the place of birth field, and you are fairly sure you know the place of birth of your individual, but not sure on age, then missing out the age field when carrying out your search will force the place of birth field to be given priority.

If a general search fails to yield results, there are still plenty of other options for you to try. Most search engines allow for you to use 'wild cards', that is, to replace one or several characters with a symbol which brings up all names that include the letters you have given in the order given. Wild cards are typically the '*' symbol, so if you entered Hig* in a surname search you would be given names including Higg, Higgett, Higginbotham, Higgins, Higgs, Higham, Higgson, and so on. Often the search engine will require you to have three letters at least before the '*' symbol, so you would not be able to use it to search names beginning with an H*. Some search engines give you the facility to use a '?' to replace a single letter, so putting in 'H?ll' would give you Hall, Hell, Hill, and Hull.

Toni's tips: *How to get the best out of a general search:*

- *The adage 'Less is More' should be applied when you are completing Search forms. The less you enter, the more results you will get. If you fill in lots of boxes then usually only one of them needs to be wrong on the census for your ancestor to be missing from the list.*

- *When undertaking a general search allow for mistakes in indexing or transcription. For example, allow a margin of 2 years either side when entering dates. Remember that on the 1841 census, the enumerator could round a person's age down by as much as 4 years so you may need to allow a greater margin.*

- *Some census service providers allow you to specify members of the household such as spouse, or parents. This can be especially useful when you need to cut down the number of results. Others have more sophisticated abilities and will allow you to search for two people in the household even if they are not related. It is worth remembering that not every member of the household was at home on census night. Individuals could be away because of their work, at school, visiting relatives or in the workhouse. The absentee would often be the head of the household, so try mixing and matching other members of the household to get the right result.*

Phonetic searches are another option, as are considering ways in which a name could have been mis-spelt. Names which usually begin with an 'H' could lose the 'H' because of the way they are said, so try searching with the second letter of the name, or names beginning with a vowel may have an 'H' put in front of them.

Kate's comment: *Common first names were often abbreviated, so that James may appear as Js or Jas. or 'Ed.' may be short for Edmund, Edwin, or Edward. Wildcard searches may help here. Some nicknames or diminutives of names may be quite different, for example, 'Maggie' for Margaret, or 'Jack' for John. A name like 'Rose' could be just that or short for Rosalind, Rosemarie, Roseanna or Rosie. Try to think creatively when looking for first names.*

If your ancestor has an unusual first name, it is possible to search under that name together with another piece of known relevant information, such as age, where he/she lived or place of birth. Or if your ancestor had a spouse, sibling or child with an unusual name, try looking for them instead, if you can locate them, you might be able to find your ancestor living with them. Some providers offer a combined household member search, e.g. a parent and child together.

If your census searches are proving fruitless, but you know your ancestor had a child around the time of the census, it may be worth obtaining a copy of the child's birth certificate as it will have an address on it which may be where the family were living at the time of the census. Some commercial providers give you the facility to search on addresses, and those that do not usually give you the facility to look through the census images for an area on a page by page basis. So it may be long-winded but you might be able to locate the family that way.

Trap 45. The family disappears

Many people using the census will at some stage find that their family seems to completely disappear from one of the censuses. As we have said before, deciphering and interpreting the information on the census is fraught with difficulties, what with poor spelling, difficult to read handwriting, and odd marks on the returns obliterating what is written there. Additionally, mistakes and misunderstandings by the enumerators add to the difficulties and frequent mis-indexing compounds the problems. Sometimes it is a wonder that anyone finds anything of use at all.

All is not lost, however. There are many reasons why a person or family is not where you expect them to be and with a bit of lateral thinking you may be able to locate them. It may simply be a case of the person you are looking for going under a different first name.

> *Kate's comment:* Nearly all of my mother's siblings went under a different name to that which they had been given at registration. I had an Uncle Ray (real name Herbert Raymond); Aunt Molly (real name Marjorie); and an Uncle Rex (real name Reginald). I did not have a clue to their real names until I started researching my family history.

In the early days of the census people usually lived in villages, but as time went by, industry in towns and cities tempted people away from their rural conditions. Once in the cities it would be harder to find your ancestors as they would become much more anonymous. Changes occurred even in major cities, for example, there was a move in London to push any smelly industries such as soap making or tanning to the east of the City where the prevailing winds would take the unpleasant aromas away. People working in those industries would have little option but to follow where the work went.

> *Toni's tip:* When you have a missing family it is sometimes better to search for the younger children as the lower the age the more likely it is to be shown correctly on the census.

There are many reasons for not being at home on the night of the census, such as the person in question being in the military or working away, or was even in a workhouse, hospital, lunatic asylum or prison. Some institutions recorded their inmates just with initial letters, but it could be that if your ancestor was in a lunatic asylum or hospital he or she may have been in no fit state to give personal details of age or place of birth. Night workers, such as a medical orderly working in a hospital would be recorded at his place of work.

"You realise you are the 37th King of England I have seen this evening?"

Kate's comment: *I had terrible problems when searching for my mother's line. Their surname was Keene, and I knew they came from a village in Wiltshire. I could not find them on every census – it seemed like one minute the whole family were there, ten years later they had gone, ten years later they were back and then ten years later they were off again. In these 'disappearing' years they were not to be found anywhere else in the country. This did not make sense – families did move away from time to time but didn't usually yo-yo between locations. Eventually the problem was solved by using first name searches. In the missing years, they had gone under the surname of Smith – which was not very helpful. Some members of later generations called themselves Keene-Smith or Smith-Keene, and it seemed as if they treated their surname as wholly interchangeable!*

People sometimes gave false information on the census forms, either for personal or political reasons. If a couple were not married the woman would be likely to use her partner's surname to avoid the stigma that would go with 'living in sin.' Names could be anglicised if their owner was from abroad, or people would change their name if they felt that by giving their true name they would be 'discovered' – they may have been in hiding for a multitude of reasons. People opposed to the census may have given false details. Some are missing from the 1911 census as they were suffragettes and were making a political point by deliberately refusing to comply with the law.

Just occasionally people were missed from the census or the actual census returns have partially or wholly gone missing, for example, parts of the 1861 census for Islington are not available.

Trap 46. The single person conundrum

Many of you who are reading this will come from a family where you have at least one sibling. In today's comparatively wealthy society in the UK, having to share a bedroom with a sibling whilst growing up is on the wane. A large proportion of children can boast their own 'space' and can get quite territorial over it. Those who can remember sharing may well have looked forward to a time where they or their brother or sister left home, and that single ownership of a bedroom would become a reality. If that was you, then be thankful that you didn't come from a Victorian family of 14, living in two rooms. It is hardly surprising that many people left the family home at a young age, not just for the chance to earn some money and relieve the financial burden on their parents, but also to have a chance of a bit of their own space.

Looking for your ancestor, after they have left the family home, can be one of the biggest difficulties a researcher will encounter. It is often details regarding the other members of the family that allow you to identify your own ancestor. Even if place of birth and age given do not match exactly with the information you have, the names and occupations of parents and siblings are clues that can confirm you have found the right person. Unless you have that desirable unusual name to chase, it can be extremely hard to locate someone during their 'going it alone' years.

This problem is illustrated by the following story: The Piggott family are looking in the 1871 census for a John Alexander Piggott, aged about 17, born in Springfield, Essex. In 1861 he was living with his parents, Thomas and Mary, in Ingatestone in the same county. In 1881 he is found as a Carman in London. His parents can be located in the 1871 census but John has by that time left home.

A painstaking research of the 1871 census has located several young men, all from Essex but none of which is an exact match to the missing John. There is a John Pigott, aged 19, born in Chelmsford and living in Colchester working as a groom; or John Piggot aged 20 born in Great Baddow, living in Ipswich, and working as a labourer; or John Piggott aged 17, born in Witham, living in South Durham and working in as a miner. But which, if any, is the right one and why is it so difficult to track him down?

It should be remembered that a young person may travel a considerable distance, to another county or even another country in order to find suitable employment. He may not have fixed on a trade or calling, for example, it was not unknown for a young son from an agricultural background to travel to distant parts to give coal mining a go for a couple of years, before deciding it is not for them. Unless your ancestor had taken up an apprenticeship, it is quite likely he would try a few different occupations before settling on one.

He may have lied about his age in order to gain employment, as a 16-year old would perhaps have been considered more able to carry out a particular job than a 14-year old, or because older people generally were paid a better wage. Once the lie had been perpetrated then he would have had to continue the deception whilst the employment lasted, particularly if he was living in the same household as his employers.

Place of birth may differ because on earlier censuses the parents would have completed the household schedule and know exactly where the child was born. However, the child may not know where precisely he was from and may well name the first place that he remembers from his childhood, or the nearest large town, or a place he thinks the enumerator might be familiar with.

All is not lost for the Piggott family. The relative in question could be missing from the census due to a simple transcription error. The exact match may be out there, waiting to be found. Family history websites generally offer an advanced search option, so if you have a similar problem you could use this to carry out a search on the first name only, plus place of birth, and age – for example: John – Springfield – 1854 (+ or – 2 years).

If this doesn't bring to light any new contenders, then look for your ancestor on all the later censuses. See what he has given as his place of birth and whether this matches any of the people on the 1871 census.

If that does not clarify things (or even if it does) you may want to try the 'negative evidence' approach, that is, to eliminate as many contenders as possible. To do this, you can get a map and determine (if you were a Piggott), precisely where Springfield is and compare it to the places of birth given by your candidates. If you were to do this you will find that John Pigott, born in Chelmsford, is the (geographically speaking) nearest match. Now you will need to see whether you can eliminate this John Pigott from your list of candidates. Can you find him with different parents on the 1861 census or find him on the 1881 census married to a different wife and children to those you would expect to see? If the answer is 'yes' to either or both of these questions, then he can be safely eliminated.

Toni's tip: Be careful not to rely purely on negative evidence. You may have eliminated all other possible entries and be left with only one contender, but this isn't necessarily the correct one and ideally you need to find other corroborative evidence. The right person may not appear on the census for a variety of reasons, such as having been completely mis-indexed, the particular section of the census on which he would have appeared has been destroyed or is missing, or he may have joined the navy and be somewhere abroad.

Sometimes there is nothing you can do at the present time to establish your ancestor's whereabouts, and although it is preferable to find your ancestors in all censuses, sometimes you just have to skip over that particular census until you uncover more evidence that helps you narrow the field.

Trap 47. Your relatives were economical with the truth

Perhaps one of the things that should surprise us is that people were generally very truthful about the information that they gave to the census enumerators. However, there is a small but significant proportion of census returnees who were, to quote the late MP Alan Clarke, 'economic with the actualité.' Before we get too critical, however, we should perhaps look at why they found it better to disguise the truth.

"Hallo luv, looking for a new frock, then?"

As discussed earlier, right from the early days of the census people were worried and suspicious, and lies were told to the enumerators out of fear of what might happen should the authorities be made aware of unregistered and illegal residents. Names were anglicised in order to suit the political environment of the time or to avoid discrimination – for example, it was not always good to have a German surname in the period running up to the First World War. Bigamists or those simply trying to flee from a former partner would change their surname in order to remain hidden.

A legacy of Poor Law regulations which stated that parishes would only look after the poor who were born in that parish, caused people to state feloniously that their birth place was the parish they were currently living in. This was out of concern that they might be removed from that parish, and sent back to their birth parish.

Whereas many people could be unsure of their exact date of birth, some people could be quite inventive about their age. If one half of a couple had increased or decreased their age to lessen an age gap between the couple, or marry when they were underage, then this subterfuge was often continued when giving details for the census. When children were registered as 'scholars' by their parents, this could have been the truth, but it could also be that the parents were breaking the law by sending their underage children out to work, and so lied. Another misleading occupation was that of dressmaker. Obviously a large number of dressmakers did exist in Victorian Britain. So did an extraordinarily large amount of prostitutes, but you won't find that occupation on many census returns. A number of sources state that it was common for prostitutes to give their occupation as dressmaker to the census enumerator, so if you find you have a dressmaker in your family, perhaps you shouldn't take that at face value!

Trap 48. You can't read what you have found

Dear old Aunt Mabel gave up her researches into the family history when she got hold of a census copy showing her grandfather's occupation as 'Porn Worker.' She was so embarrassed by this information that she fretted that the other ladies in the Mother's Union might find out her family's dark, deep secret. If only the census enumerator had used a better quality ink for recording data. He would have avoided the future distress felt by Mabel when she misread 'Farm' for 'Porn'. On the other hand, Louise Bashele of Acton might have had a much more exciting life, had she only known that on the 1861 census her occupation entry appeared to say 'Temptress' instead of the much more mundane job of 'Seamstress' that she actually held.

> *Toni's tip:* First names are often more easy to identify than surnames and these can form the basis of words that you can recognise. It also helps once you can make out a selection of words to use them as a kind of template, i.e. get to know how the writer has formed individual letters and use them as comparisons when trying to understand other words written by him. You could even create an alphabet from the letters of the words you can understand. If a name is particularly difficult to decipher then you could at least break it down to a range of names using the letters you can identify.

Misreading of entries in the 1841 census is even more likely as the enumerators often used pencil instead of ink which does not show up very well. All the censuses, however, present difficulties with legibility. This can be down to poor handwriting, the use of variable quality inks and the degradation over time of the source documents.

> **Kate's comment:** *Sometimes you can come across a census page that is startling in its clarity and is a joy to read. The next one can be a pig to decipher. Sometimes you just need to study the document until you can 'get your eye in' – in other words, you will start to get an understanding of the handwriting and begin to recognise words more easily.*

If you are working from an electronic image, you can try enlarging it as this can help enormously. If you have image enhancing software, consider changing the contrast or brightness on an image which can sharpen it enough to bring clarity.

Enumerators often used abbreviations for common names, particularly so in the 19th century, but they were not necessarily standardised abbreviations. For example, 'Thomas' may be written as either 'Thos.' or 'Th.s'. 'John' rather confusingly may be shown as 'Jn.o' or 'Jo.'. An earlier or later census may help you establish the individual's full name correctly.

There have been cases where people have thought that everyone in a household except the head of the house had the surname of 'Do', where in fact the 'Do' was short for 'Ditto', that is, all family members had the same surname as the first person on the list.

There are a couple of things to consider when trying to decipher handwriting. It should be noted that over 100 years ago, the letter 's' was often written like an 'f'. This was very often used where there would be a double s in a word such as 'Temptress.' The first 's' would be written like a 'f' and the second 's' as normal. So 'Temptress' would look like 'Temptrefs.'

What you are trying to read may be partially obscured by the writing in the line above it. Certain letters such as 'y' and 'q' have 'tails', more properly known as descenders, which can cause you problems when reading the line beneath, so try to imagine the line without those descenders from above.

If a first name is indistinguishable, then you should at least be able to ascertain the gender of that person by looking in the age column where ages are entered into either the Male or Female columns, or by their relationship to the head of the household, e.g. 'Dau' for daughter, or Sister-in-Law.

Even if every single letter can be made out, sometimes the word itself just does not make sense. It may be an unusual name, perhaps not of English derivation, such as the woman's name Wincelfled which had us scratching our heads for a while; or it could be an occupation that you had never heard of. This does not necessarily mean the word is written incorrectly, just that it is unusual, so it is worth consulting lists of old names or occupations. Try to find that person on an earlier or later census as you might have an enumerator with clearer ink or better handwriting which can confirm your interpretation.

> ***Toni's tip:*** *It is worth writing down any translations of difficult documents that you have made. You might think that after all the effort you have made you will remember at a later date what you have deciphered – but you probably won't. And you certainly won't want to go through the whole process a second time!*

Trap 49. You dismiss an entry that's not quite right

Have a look around the street or flats that you live in. Consider your neighbours, and ask yourself if any of them have experienced any changes in the last ten years. Have there been any births, marriages or deaths? Have any new people moved in? Have any of the individuals you know changed their jobs or retired? It is very unlikely that there is a single household that you know of, including your own, which has not undergone some form of change during that time period.

Ten years is a long time in anyone's life and many changes may occur to a family in the years between each census, so it pays to keep an open mind when unexpected differences are found and not to take things at face value. It is always worth looking further than just the census to try to explain these changes.

For example, there are instances of women shown on the census as being widowed, but no evidence of the death of the husband can be easily ascertained. However, a search under their 'late' husband's name in the census records may reveal them living just a few streets away. Whether the couple were estranged, and the wife liked to think that her husband was no longer living, is a matter for conjecture. It is a curiosity that in some of these cases the husband will still describe himself as married. In one instance found, the husband was living in what was then described as a lunatic asylum, which could be a reason for the wife's subterfuge!

Similarly, husbands may appear showing that they are married to someone else. It is easy to assume that the first wife must have died but it is worth checking the records for her. The husband may well have married bigamously or had moved in with another woman who would call herself his wife although not married. If the given name of the wife has not changed, but her age and/or place of birth has, then it may be that there has been a second marriage, and by coincidence the two wives have the same first name, which happens more often than you may expect.

Unexpected children may suddenly appear. You might think you have found the correct family but there is a child who is over 11 years but who does not appear on the census taken ten years earlier. It may be that you have the wrong family, which is possible if you are dealing with a common surname, but there may be other explanations. The child in question may have been staying with grandparents at the time of the earlier census. This happened quite frequently if there was a new baby in the house; older children were often sent to live with their grandparents for a time so that their mother could recover from the birth of the latest child. Or the child could have been adopted. Informal adoption of relatives or even unrelated children could occur, and sometimes parents would bring up the child of their daughter as if it was their own child. But whatever the reason, an additional child should always be investigated.

In the cases where there has been a second marriage after the first wife has died, the second wife, if a widow, may have brought children into the marriage with her. These children could take on the surname of their stepfather, so if there are unexpected older children, this may be an indication of a second marriage.

There is, of course, always the possibility that a mistake has been made. When you expect to find a family where the wife and eldest daughter of Edward are called Jane Elizabeth but the census records them both as Sarah, understandably this causes doubts that you have found the right people. In all other aspects, however, they appeared to be a perfect match for what was expected. Luckily for us, in this case a baptism entry for the daughter Jane Elizabeth showed the same address as the census which confirmed they were the right family. So the conclusion was inevitably that someone, somewhere, had made a mistake when recording the family for the census.

Toni's tip: I have found that you should always treat the given 'Relationship to Head' with some caution. An entry of 'Cousin' may not be that – they could be a nephew or niece or other kin. If a married couple are living with his parents, sometimes the couple's children are described as sons and/or daughters rather than grandchildren. I have seen cases where people described as a son-in-law or daughter-in-law are in fact stepchildren.

Trap 50. The potential of the census is not realised

It is easy to look at the census and merely take from it the obvious facts, such as ages, children's names and where each person came from. If you did just this you could be missing out on useful information or clues which can prompt the direction in which your researches should be taken.

For example, if a person disappears from a census but is in the previous one and the subsequent one – where were they on the intermediate one? The possibilities are quite wide, perhaps they could have served as a soldier or sailor (either military or merchant). They could have been a prisoner, in which case, records of their court case could be available. Perhaps the family were very poor and he or she was in the workhouse, or ill and in hospital. Perhaps he was a journeyman or apprentice for part of his working life which meant he had to work away from his family at that time. If you can establish where that person was then you may be able to find additional sources that will tell you a bit more about them, such as army or livery company records. Looking up their occupations will give you some idea of your ancestor's daily lives, the hazards they faced and how their fortunes may have varied.

Kate's comment: I was researching a family and had the problem whereby one person is missing off the 1901 census. I did eventually find him – as an inmate in a lunatic asylum. As he is shown living with his family and working on the 1911 census I can only assume he was one of the lucky people who made a recovery from his illness.

Some censuses can tell you diverse information such as to the general health of the individual, such as 'Blind' or the rather harsh 'Imbecile from Birth.' Another can tell you whether the person worked for someone (i.e. 'Worker') or had their own business (i.e. 'Employer'). From the 1891 census, you can see how many rooms the family lived in, which can give you an indication of the relative wealth of the family at that time. If you see the word 'Ind.' or 'Independent' under occupation, this may suggest that they were sufficiently wealthy that they did not have to work. You can also establish if they lived in shared accommodation or occupied the whole dwelling. This is indicated by either a single or double stroke / or //. A double stroke // means that it is a complete list of people in a dwelling; a single stroke / was used to divide different households sharing a dwelling.

If your family lived in London in the late 19th century, you may be able to find their addresses on the Booth poverty map, which will give you an idea of their social and economic status. Charles Booth surveyed life and labour in London between 1886 and 1903. He categorised streets somewhat bluntly, for example, your ancestors may have come from an area described by Booth as housing people who were the 'Lowest class – vicious, semi-criminal,' regardless of what individual people were like. His colour-coded map, survey notes and data can be found on-line, and is an excellent and under-used resource.

People living in a household but described as visitor or boarder may in fact be a family member, for example, the wife's sister or mother, and whose name can give you a clue to the wife's maiden name. A good indication of a potential sister is if the age gap between the visitor and the wife is not very wide, and if they both come from the same area.

Toni's tip: Use the information found on the census to carry out some general Internet searching. For example, if your ancestor's surname was Brewster, if he lived in Plaistow and worked as a butcher, put in terms such as 'Brewster Plaistow Butcher' in the search engine. Sometimes if you are lucky you can get some unexpected information this way which helps you build a bigger picture of your ancestor.

If you take a meander through surrounding census entries to look at the neighbourhood, you may discover interesting connections. You can often find intermarriage between neighbours, witnesses of marriages, or even parents or siblings living next door or in the same road. Although if you were in a Welsh village and where nearly everyone had the surname Jones, you would have a challenge on your hands to sort out who was related to whom!

...and finally

If you have enjoyed this book, you might want to read its companion volume "Grandad Was A Dwarf Strangler: 50 More Family History Traps", a useful volume which will guide you through the trips and spills associated with using record offices and other archives; website-based challenges, finding missing ancestors, presenting your findings and much more. Written in our distinctive style and packed with tips and comments, and illustrated with cartoons to make you smile, plus all you ever really needed to know about ancestral dwarf-stranglers.